BIRDHOUSES & FEEDERS
YOU CAN MAKE

Complete Plans and Instructions for Bird-Friendly Nesting and Feeding Sites

PAUL GERHARDS

STACKPOLE
BOOKS

Special thanks to consultants Susan and Richard Day for their expert advice.

Copyright ©1999 by Paul Gerhards

Published by
STACKPOLE BOOKS
5067 Ritter Road
Mechanicsburg, PA 17055
www.stackpolebooks.com

Printed in the United States of America

10 9 8 7 6 5 4 3

FIRST EDITION

Cover design by Caroline Stover
Cover and interior photographs by Patrick Gerhards

Library of Congress Cataloging-in-Publication Data

Gerhards, Paul.
    Birdhouses and feeders you can make: complete plans and instructions for bird-friendly nesting and feeding sites/Paul Gerhards.—1st ed.
      p.   cm.
    Includes bibliographical references.
    ISBN 0–8117–2679–7
    1. Birdhouses—Design and construction. 2. Bird feeders—Design and construction. I. Title.
QL676.5.G47 1999
6901'.8927—dc21   98–27505
                                                    CIP

BIRDHOUSES & FEEDERS

YOU CAN MAKE

Also by Paul Gerhards

Entertainment Centers You Can Make
Garden Structures You Can Make
Backyard Play Areas You Can Make
Children's Furniture You Can Make
How to Sell What You Make

CONTENTS

Introduction
vii

Birding Basics
1

Birdhouse Basics
5

Birdhouse Projects

Bird Feeder Basics
57

Bird Feeder Projects

Bibliography
82

Metric Conversions
83

Index
84

INTRODUCTION

Walk into just about any gift shop, flip through the latest decorator magazine, and you'll be sure to see at least one birdhouse. But chances are these birdhouses have less to do with attracting nesting pairs of birds than with adding a bright spot of color to a garden or livening up the mantle in the den.

No doubt about it, birdhouses are hot decorating items. Unfortunately, many of these decorator birdhouses, no matter how attractive they are to us, are not at all attractive to birds. If your intentions are to attract birds to your backyard, whether for nesting or feeding, you'll need a house that's suitable for the purpose. The projects in this book are all intended to be functional rather than simply decorative birdhouses.

Birdhouses and bird feeders are among the most rewarding weekend woodworking projects. They are small and simple, and the beginning woodworker will have no trouble producing a functional item on the first attempt. And these are excellent family projects. With supervision, even a small child can assemble and finish a nestbox or feeder he or she can be proud of.

The most important reason for putting up birdhouses and feeders is to provide nesting and feeding sites. With development eroding much of their natural habitat, many bird species need our help. Birds are a key ecological element, helping keep insect and rodent populations in check. Birdhouses can provide safe havens for species that are endangered and faced with possible extinction. The bluebird is a good example. By 1950, populations of all three species—western, eastern, and mountain—were nearly wiped out by the destruction of their natural habitats and extensive use of pesticides. Thanks to the persistent and patient efforts of bluebird enthusiasts, who placed networks of nestboxes all over the country, numbers have rebounded and the bluebird is once again a common sight in most parts of the country.

Another benefit of putting up birdhouses and feeders is watching the birds that come to use them. With a good field guide, you can learn to identify the birds in your area. Being able to recognize a little gray bird as a Tufted Titmouse or a White-breasted Nuthatch is fun, and once you come to know your local birds, they seem like old friends.

And birdsong is one of the most pleasant aspects of nature. For me, the harbinger of spring, more so than the return of the robins, is the rolling morning chorus produced by a multitude of birds as they begin each day by reestablishing their territories.

Building your own houses and feeders will enable you to play a part in this grand scheme of nature.

BIRDING BASICS

Attracting birds to your backyard birdhouses is a lot like fishing. First, you need a general idea of what kinds of fish you're likely to catch. You probably won't find steelhead in that pond on the lower forty of the old homestead. Second, you need the right gear. No use trying to catch catfish with a fly rod. Third, you need plenty of patience. Don't expect the fish to jump into the boat all by itself.

It's easy for a would-be avian landlord to make the above fishing mistakes. A novice birder often chooses a birdhouse based on how it looks rather than on how it will function. Birds don't judge houses by our concept of cuteness but select a nest site based on criteria much different from ours.

Another mistake is improper placement. The instinct in birds to reproduce is strong, and a mating pair will always find a place for a nest. But just because you hang a box in a tree doesn't necessarily mean a mating pair will choose it. The box must be placed the right height above the ground and in the right habitat. There must be a clear path to the entrance. Are there other mating pairs of the same species nearby? Some species are very territorial, and a mating pair will not allow others to nest within a certain radius of their own nest.

THE KINDS OF BIRDS YOU CAN EXPECT TO ATTRACT

Perhaps the most important question is this: Is the house you've put up closely matched to the bird species you want to nest there? I don't mean to imply that only one type of bird will nest in only one kind of house. On the other hand, you won't get a bluebird to nest in a house designed for a Wood Duck. And you won't get a cardi-nal to nest in any birdhouse, because a cardinal is not a cavity nester.

Cavity Nesters

In North America, there are some 650 species of birds. Of those, only about 85 are cavity nesters. A cavity-nesting bird is one that builds a nest within an enclosed space, be it a hollow in a tree trunk, a nestbox, or an old shoe. All the other species build their nests in the open, although they usually camouflage them. It's interesting to note that whereas only 20 to 40 percent of noncavity nests succeed, the percentage of successful cavity nests is between 60 and 80. It's one of nature's mysteries that just 13 percent of North America's bird species use the more successful mode of raising their young.

Primary Cavity Nesters

Cavity-nesting birds are grouped into two categories: primary and secondary. Primary cavity nesters are those birds that excavate their own nesting sites by chiseling into trunks and branches with their beaks: the woodpeckers. Because this is an instinctive part of the mating ritual, it's difficult to attract primary cavity nesters to a birdhouse. Nevertheless, some birders have successfully attracted woodpeckers by stuffing nestboxes with sawdust, thus allowing the birds to do what comes naturally before moving in. It's worth a try.

Secondary Cavity Nesters

Secondary cavity nesters are those birds that build nests in most any available cavity, including those made by primary cavity nesters and those made by humans. Each species has its own set of requirements that precludes

TABLE 1

CAVITY NESTERS THAT MAY USE BIRDHOUSES OR NESTBOXES

Bluebirds
  Eastern Bluebird
  Mountain Bluebird
  Western Bluebird
Chickadees
  Black-capped Chickadee
  Carolina Chickadee
  Chestnut-backed Chickadee
  Mountain Chickadee
Ducks
  Barrow's Goldeneye
  Bufflehead
  Common Goldeneye
  Common Merganser

  Hooded Merganser
  Wood Duck
Finches
  House Finch
Flycatchers
  Ash-throated Flycatcher
  Great Crested Flycatcher
Nuthatches
  Red-breasted Nuthatch
  White-breasted Nuthatch
Raptors
  American Kestrel
  Barn Owl
  Barred Owl

  Eastern Screech Owl
  Northern Saw-whet Owl
  Western Screech Owl
Swallows
  Purple Martin
  Tree Swallow
  Violet-green Swallow
Titmice
  Plain Titmouse
  Tufted Titmouse
Warblers
  Prothonotary Warbler
Woodpeckers
  Downy Woodpecker

  Golden-fronted Woodpecker
  Hairy Woodpecker
  Northern Flicker
  Red-bellied Woodpecker
  Red-headed Woodpecker
Wrens
  Carolina Wren
  Bewick's Wren
  House Wren
Other
  House Sparrow
  Starling

---

dozens of sites. Table 1 lists forty-one cavity nesters most likely to be attracted to birdhouses and nestboxes.

Platform Nesters

Some noncavity nesters are platform nesters, birds that build nests on solid, relatively open surfaces. You'll find such nests under bridges and eaves and on beams in a carport. An unfortunate place to find such a nest is atop the porch light near your front door. Although it might be fun to have chirping babies so close by, the mess they make is not so fun.

I've kept this category of birds separate from the other noncavity nesters because you can construct simple platforms on which these birds may nest. Plans for three kinds of platforms follow the birdhouse plans. Perhaps you'll attract a pair of one or more of these birds: American Robin, Barn Swallow, Black Phoebe, Cliff Swallow, Eastern Phoebe, or Say's Phoebe.

Other Noncavity Nesters

If your goal is to attract as many nesting pairs of birds to your backyard as possible, you are not limited to cavity nesters. Birds nest in trees, shrubs, and brush, and on the ground. Depending on where your backyard is, how big it is, and what kinds of habitat you have or can make available, you might be able to attract mating pairs of the birds listed in Table 2.

RANGE, HABITAT, AND TERRITORY

Range, habitat, and territory are important factors in determining what birds you can expect to attract to your birdhouses. Range refers to the larger geographical area a species will occupy. Depending on the bird, a range might cover a good portion of North America or just a small corner of one state. Many birds are year-round residents throughout their entire range. Others move to different areas of the country during winter and summer. A good bird field guide will show you the ranges of the various species. If you live outside the range of a given bird, don't expect to attract a pair to your backyard.

Habitat refers to the specific qualities of a species' natural environment. Habitats include forests, wetlands, and open areas. A bird's range might be large, but where you will find that bird within a given range is governed by its habitat needs. Habitats often overlap, and many species thrive on the edge where two or more habitats come together. This is a benefit for birders who live in the suburbs, where the mix of shrubs, trees, and lawns provides plenty of edge habitat and attracts an abundance of such birds.

When it comes to breeding, birds also have territories. Once a nesting pair selects a site, the birds protect that space from encroachment not only by potential predators, but also by other members of their own species.

The size of the territory differs among species. A single pair of chickadees, for example, requires about 10 acres. If a nearby neighbor has a breeding pair in his backyard, you might attract these little black-capped birds to your backyard feeder, but you probably won't get a mating pair to nest. But you'll never know until you try.

Many birds don't recognize the boundaries of other species. And some birds, like some species of swallows, are communal and nest in colonies.

Keep all this in mind when placing birdhouses in hopes of attracting a specific kind of bird. If you live in the country on a large parcel of land that includes a variety of habitat types, you may have a little more control over what tenants you will attract. But again it's similar to fishing, where you have relatively little say over what fish will bite.

BIRD IDENTIFICATION
A good field guide will help you identify your neighborhood birds. These books are available at bookstores, bird shops, and from your local chapter of the Audubon Society. How the book is organized is important; a good field guide allows you to quickly identify the species in question. Read the introductory material on how to use the guide. It will help you get acquainted with the book and give you an idea of the ease of using it.

Some field guides use photographs of the birds; others use paintings. At first glance photographs might seem preferable, but this isn't necessarily the case when trying to identify a bird. A photograph depicts a particular bird at a particular time in a particular locale. But the characteristics of different birds of any given species vary. The paintings show the important distinguishing characteristics of each species, which is a great aid in identification.

MAKING OBSERVATIONS
Whether you've put out one nestbox or a dozen, you'll want to make some observations and perhaps monitor your tenants' progress as they brood their young. If you're statistically inclined, you might wish to keep careful notes from year to year. This information will let you evaluate the attributes of one birdhouse over another.

The first thing to watch for is when a mating pair begins showing interest in one of your birdhouses. Make note of the date and conditions. If you don't already know the species, make an identification. In many species, the male is more colorful than the female. Try to determine which is which and who does what work.

TABLE 2
NONCAVITY NESTERS THAT MAY NEST IN YOUR BACKYARD

On the Ground	In Shrubs		Great-tailed Grackle
American Black Duck	Brown Thrasher	Black-billed Magpie	Hooded Oriole
American Woodcock	California Thrasher	Brewer's Blackbird	Inca Dove
Bobwhite	Canyon Towhee	Eastern Kingbird	Lesser Goldfinch
Bobolink	Chipping Sparrow	Red-eyed Vireo	Mourning Dove
California Quail	Common Yellowthroat	Rose-breasted Grosbeak	Northwestern Crow
Canada Goose	Gray Catbird	Western Kingbird	Orchard Oriole
Common Ground-Dove	Indigo Bunting	Wood Thrush	Pine Siskin
Eastern Meadowlark	Northern Cardinal	Yellow-billed Cuckoo	Purple Finch
Killdeer	Northern Mockingbird	**In Trees**	Red-tailed Hawk
Mallard	Red-winged Blackbird	American Crow	Scarlet Tanager
Ring-necked Pheasant	Song Sparrow	Baltimore Oriole	Summer Tanager
Rufous-sided Towhee	Yellow Warbler	Blue Jay	Western Tanager
Western Meadowlark	**In Shrubs or Trees**	Cedar Waxwing	Western Wood Pewee
White-crowned Sparrow	American Robin	Common Grackle	
White-throated Sparrow	Black-billed Cuckoo	Eastern Wood Pewee	
		Great Horned Owl	

House # _____   Year_____

Species _____

Date nest building begins _____   Date laying begins _____

Number of eggs in clutch _____   Date incubation begins _____

Number of eggs hatched _____   Date of first fledge _____

Number of fledglings _____   Date of last fledge _____

Other observations _____

_____

_____

_____

_____

You might want to record your bird observations on a monitoring card.

The birds will begin to mate during nest-building activities. When the nest is finished, the female will lay eggs daily until the clutch is complete. Only then will she start incubating the eggs. The number of eggs in a clutch depends on the species.

Check the progress of the nest periodically to determine when laying and incubation begin. If possible, wait until both parents are away to make your inspections. Tap lightly on the box before opening it. If an adult bird is inside, this gives it a chance to leave. If the brooding bird doesn't leave, carefully open the box, make your observations, then quietly close the box.

It's an old story, and one that still might be argued now and then, that adult birds will abandon a nest touched by humans. This isn't necessarily true. Birds have a poor sense of smell, and even if they do see you inspect the nest, it's unlikely they'll abandon it.

Nevertheless, you should avoid making inspections during incubation; during bad weather, which could endanger nestlings; and in the three or four days before the nestlings fledge. To determine when this occurs, you need to know how long the nestling stage is. Refer to a guidebook to learn incubation and nesting days, as this varies with different species. If in doubt, save the inspections for later.

You'll know that the eggs have hatched when the parents start making relentless excursions for food. Observe which of the parents brings the food. Sometimes they take turns brooding and food gathering. Once the nestlings have fledged, they are better able to regulate their own body temperature and care for themselves.

When the baby birds have grown their flight feathers and left the nest, they are no longer nestlings but fledglings. This does not mean, however, that they are ready to be on their own. Fledglings might depend on their parents to bring them food for several weeks before they become competent fliers and food gatherers.

BIRDHOUSE BASICS

Birdhouse building doesn't take a lot of skill nor does it require expensive materials and tools. With a little practice and attention to details you can build a fine collection of birdhouses in just a few weekends.

Before constructing your birdhouses, it's necessary to take into account a few other factors, such as where and how to mount your birdhouses and how to guard against predators.

SITE SELECTION

Selecting sites for your birdhouses is not an exacting science. In the wild, birds will nest where they can. Yet some consideration of placement is still necessary.

Birdhouses should be mounted away from human traffic areas. Though you want to be able to view the comings and goings of the birds, the nestboxes should not be so close that the birds will be continually frightened away. Also, birds are not very considerate about where they leave their droppings.

When locating a birdhouse, choose a place with a clear, unobstructed path to the entry hole. Birds need an easy way in and out of their nestboxes. If possible, the entrance should face away from prevailing winds. Most birds also need a place nearby for perching so that they can keep an eye out for predators and wait for their mates to finish feeding the nestlings.

MOUNTING THE BIRDHOUSE

Birdhouses can be mounted in several ways. They can be placed atop a post or hung against it, fixed to a tree or hung from a branch, or fastened to the side of your house, barn, or storage shed. How you mount your birdhouses depends, in part, on the style of the house itself.

I recommend using screws instead of nails for mounting. Screws are much easier to remove than nails, and when you take the house down for cleaning or repair, screws cause less wear and tear on both the birdhouse and the surface to which it's attached. Use a length of stiff wire, chain, or nylon cord to suspend a birdhouse from a branch. A hanging house should be reasonably secure so that it will not spin or bang into other branches in the wind.

PROVIDING NESTING MATERIAL

Different species have different preferences for nesting materials, but on the whole, birds incorporate all types of things into their nests. To help your prospective tenants, you can place a selection of such items in plain sight. Pieces of string and yarn 5 or 6 inches long, bits of cloth, and fur are all good things to put out. Drape these items over the branches of a tree or shrub, or put them in a string bag, suet holder, or basket, and hang it from a tree.

Mud is a necessary building material of some birds, such as barn swallows and robins. If the weather is continually dry during nesting season, try to maintain a patch of mud for the birds to use. And it's always a good idea to provide birdbaths or shallow pools of clean water for birds to drink and bathe in.

PROTECTION FROM PREDATORS, PARASITES, AND COMPETITORS

Once you've established yourself as a landlord, you have a certain responsibility to protect your tenants. After all,

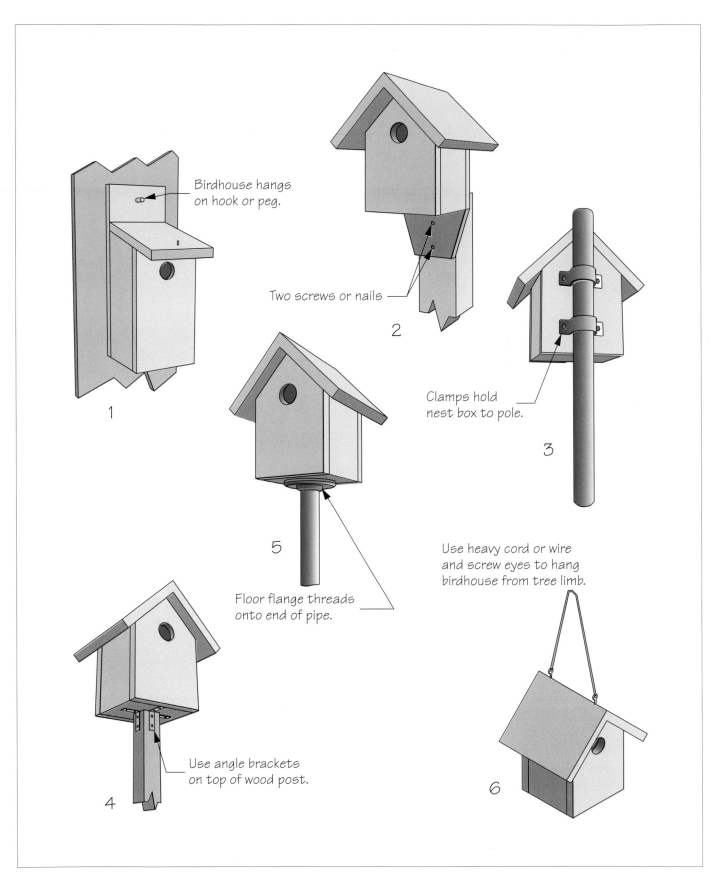

Birdhouse hangs on hook or peg.

Two screws or nails

1

2

Clamps hold nest box to pole.

3

5

Floor flange threads onto end of pipe.

Use heavy cord or wire and screw eyes to hang birdhouse from tree limb.

Use angle brackets on top of wood post.

4

6

Six ways to mount or hang a birdhouse.

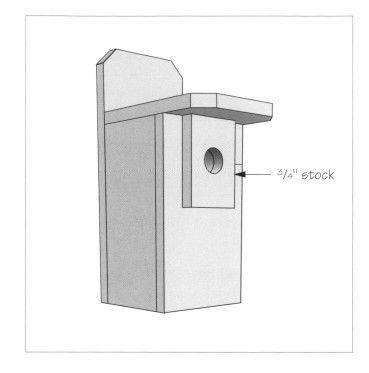

3/4" stock

Add a piece of ³/₄-inch wood to the entry to make it more difficult for predators to reach in.

what good is it to put up birdhouses and nestboxes if they will be ravaged by predators? Your ability to forestall predation can give nesting birds an advantage.

The most common predators are raccoons, cats, squirrels, rats, mice, and in some areas, snakes. You can't protect nests from all predators all the time, but by investing a little extra time and materials, you can increase the chances that your nestlings will fledge.

You can make it more difficult for raccoons and cats to reach into a nestbox by increasing the thickness of the entrance hole: Add a piece of ³/₄-inch stock to the front. Other methods of discouraging predators from reaching in, such as extending the opening with a length of tubing or wire mesh, might also discourage birds from investigating a potential nesting site. If the birdhouse is hung or mounted on a tree or wood post, a well-sloped roof with about a 3-inch overhang will discourage or even prevent predators from reaching in from the top.

If you find that an entry hole has been enlarged by chewing, a squirrel is the likely culprit. You can overlay the entrance with a piece of sheet metal with the right diameter hole cut into it, but be certain the edges are smooth.

An effective way to keep predators from climbing a tree on which a birdhouse is mounted is to wrap the trunk with a sheet metal sleeve 2 or 3 feet wide. Secure the sheet metal with screws so that you can easily remove and loosen it as years go by. Paint the sleeve a dull green or brown so that it will blend in with the surroundings. This method works only if there is no other access to the tree from another tree, rooftop, wall, or other structure nearby.

Metal poles are better than wood posts because animals can't get their claws into metal. But if the pole is too narrow, some animals might be able to get a grip around the pole and shinny up it. Slip a piece of 4- or 6-inch-diameter PVC pipe around the pole before mounting the birdhouse on top. The pipe should reach nearly to the bottom of the house.

You can also fit the pole or post with a cone-shaped predator guard made of sheet metal to keep predators at bay. Make a pattern from a large piece of stiff paper or

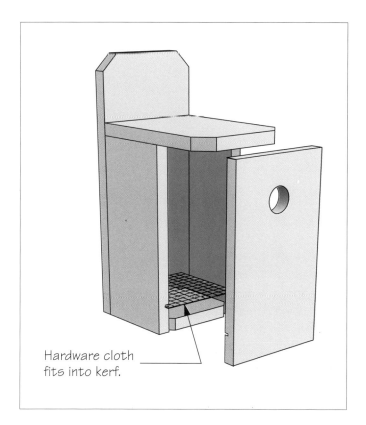

Hardware cloth fits into kerf.

A raised floor made of hardware cloth can help screen out blowfly larvae. Cut a saw kerf about ¹/₄ inch deep in the sides and 1 inch above the bottom. Insert the hardware cloth into the kerf.

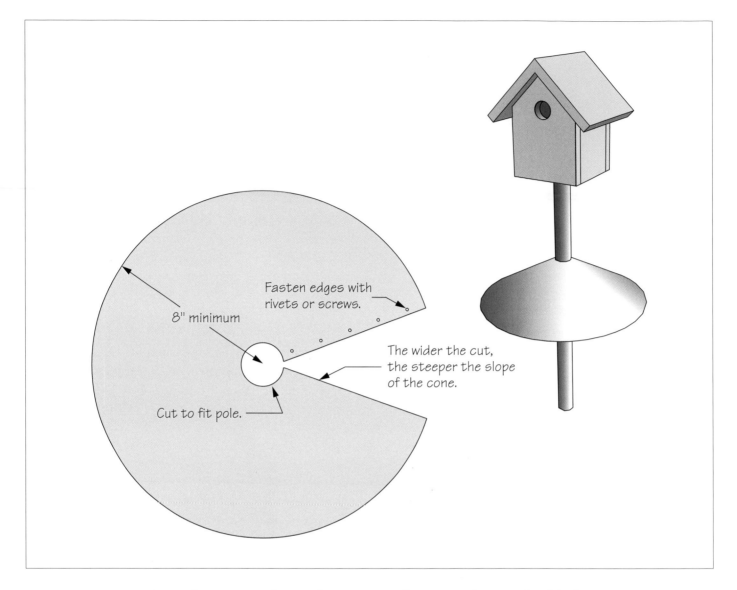

Fasten edges with
rivets or screws.

8" minimum

The wider the cut,
the steeper the slope
of the cone.

Cut to fit pole.

A predator guard can deter pests from getting to the birds.

cardboard to get the shape you want. Trace the pattern onto a piece of sheet metal, cut it out with sheet-metal shears, and file down the sharp edges. Use sheet-metal screws, rivets, or small nuts and bolts to hold the cone together. Slip the cone over the pole before mounting the birdhouse. To keep the cone in place on a metal pole, use a hose clamp underneath it.

Parasites can be just as much of a problem in a back-yard birdhouse as they are in a natural cavity. The most common parasites are blowfly larvae and mites. Experts disagree on the best way to treat these pests. Some say that treating the nests with pyrethrin or rotenone is acceptable; others say pesticides should never be used because of the effects they might have on the birds. Whether to use these chemicals is up to you. A raised

floor of ¹/₄-inch hardware cloth can help screen out blowfly larvae.

Wasps and yellow jackets may also invade your bird-houses. Rub the underside of the roof and the upper portions of the walls with bar soap or petroleum jelly to prevent these insects from building a nest.

Competition among species that require similar nesting sites, as well as among birds of the same species, is common. It's best to leave well enough alone. In fact, with certain exceptions, birds are protected by federal and state laws. There are, however, two exceptions: Sparrows (also known as English Sparrows) and starlings. These are non-native birds and are not protected under the law. Both species are fiercely competitive and will even invade an existing nest site and kill the occupants. Because starlings and House Sparrows are not protected by law, the best way to prevent them from nesting in one of your boxes is to persistently remove their nests. If another species doesn't soon occupy the birdhouse, try relocating it. This assumes, of course, that you do not want starlings or House Sparrows to nest. If your goal is to attract *any* nesting pair of birds—perhaps to allow your youngster to observe the nesting process—by all means let them be.

CLEANING AND MAINTENANCE

Like almost anything else, birdhouses require basic maintenance and cleaning. Check your nestboxes in the fall so that they can be ready for the next season. Make sure that hinges are working smoothly and the structure is still sound. Give the outside another coat of paint or stain if necessary. Some people leave the boxes down until early spring or plug the entry holes to prevent mice or rats from nesting inside. If you leave the boxes out, however, overwintering birds may use them for roosting.

There has been some debate over whether to discard old nests. Some say yes; others say it's not necessary unless the nest is infested with vermin. If you've put out several boxes, try leaving some nests intact. Include your observations in your monitoring notes. One way or the other, you should remove wasp nests or anything else that shouldn't be there.

MATERIALS

The birdhouses described in this book are made of wood. What kind of wood you use depends on what's available locally. Softwoods like white pine, Douglas fir, redwood, and western red cedar are good choices; redwood and cedar are preferable because they better withstand weathering. Hardwoods are more expensive and more difficult to work with, so they are not particularly good choices for weekend birdhouse projects.

Solid-wood boards—that is, wood other than sheet goods like plywood—come off the shelf in $3/4$-inch thicknesses and widths of $3^1/2$, $5^1/2$, $7^1/2$, $9^1/2$, and $11^1/2$ inches. With one exception, all of the birdhouses I've included in this book are drawn using $3/4$-inch boards for all the components. This is known as 1× stock, as in 1×4 and 1×6. They are easy to join and have good insulating qualities, although thinner boards may be used if that's what you have on hand. Just adjust the dimensions accordingly.

Half-inch and $3/4$-inch exterior-grade fir plywood are also good choices, especially for the larger nest boxes for owls and ducks. You also can use $1/2$-inch wafer board ($7/16$-inch actual) or oriented strand board (OSB). Although exterior grade, these products will last longer if painted. Unfinished, they are not very attractive.

I don't recommend using $1/4$-inch or $3/8$-inch plywood for all of the components of a birdhouse, yet these thicknesses are useful for some of the components. The chief concern is the strength and integrity of a given joint. It's difficult to get a good, solid corner by fastening together two pieces of $1/4$-inch plywood. On the other hand, fastening a piece of $1/4$-inch plywood to the edge of a piece of $3/4$-inch plywood will yield a solid corner. In this case, however, you'll need to first bore pilot holes to avoid splitting the wood.

If you're frugal, you can make dozens of birdhouses and feeders from scrap wood. Some of the birdhouses described in this book were made from old fence boards, $5/8$ and $3/4$ inch thick.

Cedar shingles and shakes are excellent for siding and roofing, if they are adhered in such a way that won't harm birds inside—that is, with no nails or staples poking through to the inside. Use a good exterior adhesive to glue small pieces into place. You can further decorate a birdhouse with materials like twigs, strips of bark, and bits of moss to create a natural look.

Fasteners and other hardware should be galvanized, zinc plated, or otherwise rated for outdoor use. To assemble the birdhouses and feeders, you can use nails, screws, or both. I prefer screws because they can be driven and removed easily without damaging the house.

I once saw an interesting collection of birdhouses for sale at a crafts fair. The crafter made excellent use of old license plates and pieces of corrugated metal for the roofs. Unfortunately, this isn't so good for the birds, as the conductive qualities of the metal will turn the birdhouse into an oven in the hot sun.

An exception to the use of metal is for Purple Martin houses, some of which are made from aluminum and painted white to reflect the heat. Martin houses can also be fashioned from white, 6-inch-diameter PVC pipe or made by suspending a group of gourds with holes cut in them from a frame with wire or string.

Most wooden birdhouses will last longer if you apply a finish to the outside. Cedar or redwood houses, however, will last many years, even if left unfinished. If you choose to paint or stain your birdhouse, use flat, muted earth tones—colors that will blend into the scenery. Glossy or flashy colors will likely scare away potential tenants. Dark paints are potentially dangerous to birds, as they can cause a heat buildup inside the box. Never apply a finish to the inside of the house, and never use wood preservatives; the chemicals could be harmful to the birds.

TOOLS

As with any woodworking project, unless you're working with precut pieces, some cutting of the wood is necessary. I'm assuming some knowledge of and ability with woodworking tools. If you're a beginner, refer to a general woodworking text for the basics. The most important consideration is safety when using power tools.

To cut clean, round entrance holes in the birdhouses, a hole saw works well. These come in several standard sizes and can be used with an electric drill.

Modern adjustable hole cutters are also available, but read the label before buying; some of these cutters must be used with a drill press. You can also use an old-fashioned adjustable bit with a brace, if you're lucky enough to own or find one of these relics. You can cut the larger elliptical holes with a jigsaw.

Another valuable tool to have on hand is a cordless drill. This makes mounting, dismounting, and opening houses for cleaning a snap, especially out in the field.

THE RIGHT BOX FOR THE RIGHT BIRD

Secondary cavity nesters have been nesting in natural sites for thousands of years, so it would seem that any box of the shop-made variety should work fine. But this

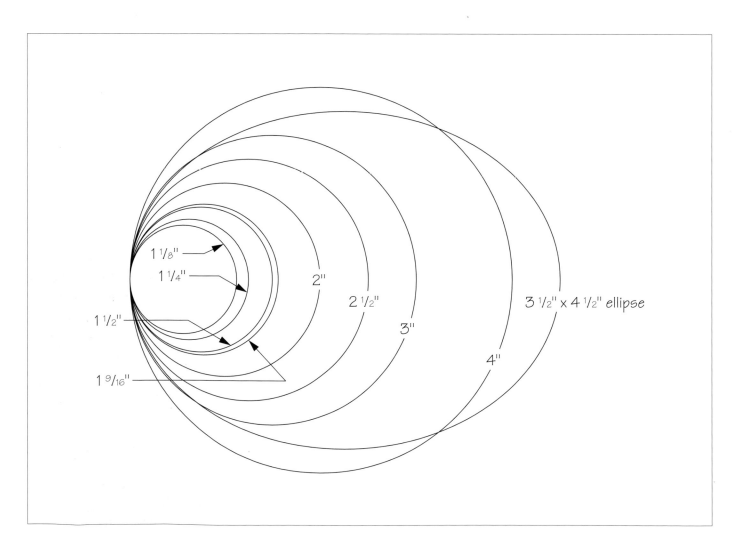

1 1/8"
1 1/4"
2"
2 1/2"
3 1/2" x 4 1/2" ellipse
1 1/2"
3"
1 9/16"
4"

Relative entrance sizes.

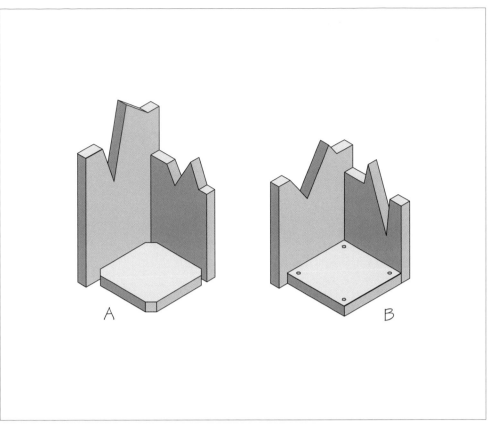

Two methods for providing drainage.
In A, the corners of the floor are lopped off. In B,
four ¹/₄-inch holes are bored through the floor.

is not necessarily so. Birds are very particular creatures, but they are governed more by instinct than taste. Decades of bird-watching and experimentation with nestboxes have yielded several successful designs.

There are two primary criteria that determine which kinds of birds will likely choose to nest inside a particular birdhouse: the interior dimensions and the size and placement of the entrance hole. There are other details that go toward making an ideal nestbox but are not species-specific. Table 3 lists the cavity-nesting birds and gives guidelines for houses for each species.

The birdhouses in this book are designs that have proven successful. And most of them can be used to attract a variety of species, the limiting factor being the size of the entrance hole. Only one house has a proper name attached to it: the Peterson house, designed by Dick Peterson especially for bluebirds. This is not to say that a Peterson house won't attract other species, say, a pair of chickadees.

ENTRANCE HOLES

If the size of a birdhouse or nest box is a determining factor in what kinds of birds will brood inside, the size and placement of the entrance hole is even more important. An entrance that is too small excludes most birds—all of them if it's less than $1\frac{1}{8}$ inches in diameter. Of all the cavity nesters, most chickadees and house wrens can make use of an entry that is $1\frac{1}{8}$ inches. In the wild, however, these birds wouldn't likely find such a small entrance because they are secondary cavity nesters, dependent on the industry of the primary cavity nesters. The smallest bird-made entry hole, at $1\frac{1}{4}$ inches, is that of the Downy Woodpecker.

So why not make the hole $2\frac{1}{2}$ inches in diameter and, at the same time, make the floor area of the box 6×6 inches to accommodate all the smaller birds? First, some birds prefer a smaller hole. Second, you'll probably want to attract only certain birds and exclude other birds—namely, starlings and House Sparrows.

TABLE 3
Nestbox Specifications and General Habitat Considerations for Cavity-Nesting Birds

Bird	Interior Dimensions (inches)	Height of Box (inches)	Entrance Diameter (inches)	Height of Entrance above Floor (inches)	Height to Mount Box above Ground (feet)	General Habitat
Bluebirds						
Eastern Bluebird	4x4–5x5	8–12	1½	6–7	5–10	Open fields with scattered trees, edges.
Mountain Bluebird	5x5–5½x5	11–12	1 9/16	6–7	5–10	Open forests 5,000 to 11,000 feet in elevation.
Western Bluebird	5x5	8–12	1½–1 9/16	6–7	5–10	Open forests.
Chickadees						
Black-capped Chickadee	4x4–5x5	8–12	1⅛–1½	6–8	6–15	Brush edges and forests.
Carolina Chickadee	4x4–5x5	8–12	1⅛–1½	6–8	6–15	Brush edges, southeastern forests.
Chestnut-backed Chickadee	4x4–5x5	8–12	1⅛–1½	6–8	6–15	Northwestern coastal forests.
Mountain Chickadee	4x4–5x5	8–12	1⅛–1½	6–8	6–15	Evergreen forests 6,000 to 11,000 feet in elevation.
Ducks						
Barrow's Goldeneye	10x10–12x12	24	3½x4½ horiz. ellipse	16–18	15–20	Within 100 feet of small to medium lakes.
Bufflehead	6x6–7x7	16–19	3	14–18	5–15	Nests on or over small ponds and lakes edged with open woodlands.
Common Goldeneye	10x10–12x12	24	3½x4½ horiz. ellipse	16–18	15–20	Forested lakes and rivers.
Common Merganser	10x10–12x12	24–34	5x6 horiz. ellipse	16–20	8–20	Northern and western wetlands.
Hooded Merganser	10x10–12x12	24	3x4 horiz. ellipse	16–18	5–20	Wooded streams and lakes.
Wood Duck	10x10–12x12	24	3x4 horiz. ellipse	16–20	5–25	Bottomland deciduous forests near water.
Finches						
House Finch	4x4–6x6	6–12	1⅜–2	4–7	8–12	Backyards, suburbs, canyons, ranches.
Flycatchers						
Ash-throated Flycatcher	4x4–6x6	8–12	1½–2½	6–7	8–20	Western deciduous open woods and edges, mesquite, saguaros.
Great Crested Flycatcher	4x4–6x6	9–12	1½–2½	6–8	8–20	Forest-field edges.
Nuthatches						
Red-breasted Nuthatch	4x4–5x5	9–12	1⅛–1½	6–7	5–20	Coniferous forests.
White-breasted Nuthatch	4x4–5x5	9–12	1⅛–1½	6–7	5–20	Deciduous wooded areas.

Continued

Bird	Interior Dimensions (inches)	Height of Box (inches)	Entrance Diameter (inches)	Height of Entrance above Floor (inches)	Height to Mount Box above Ground (feet)	General Habitat
Raptors						
American Kestrel	8x8–9x9	12–18	3	9–12	10–30	Open and semiopen countryside.
Barn Owl	10 w x 18 d–16 w x 22 d	15–18	6–8	4	12–18	Forests, farms, marshes, fields.
Barred Owl	14x14	16–28	6–8	12–18		Southern swamps, moist bottomland forests.
Eastern Screech Owl	6x6–8x8	12–18	2½–4	9–12	10–30	Open forests and meadow edges, farmlands, orchards.
Northern Saw-whet Owl	6x6–8x8	12–18	2½–4	9–12	12–20	Northern forests.
Western Screech Owl	6x6–8x8	12–18	2½–4	9–12	10–30	Open forests and meadow edges, farmlands, orchards.
Swallows						
Purple Martin	6x6	6	2–2½	1	15–20	Open countryside near water. Communal nesters.
Tree Swallow	4x4–5x5	6–12	1½	1–7	5–15	Open countryside near water.
Violet-green Swallow	4x4–5x5	6–12	1½	1–7	5–15	Open woodlands and forest edges.
Titmice						
Plain Titmouse	4x4–5x5	8–12	1¼–1½	6–8	6–15	Oak and pinyon-juniper woodlands.
Tufted Titmouse	4x4–5x5	8–12	1¼–1½	6–8	6–15	Eastern deciduous woodlands.
Warblers						
Prothonotary Warbler	4x4–5x5	8–12	1¼–1½	5–7	5–12	Swamps and wetlands in Eastern deciduous forests.
Woodpeckers						
Downy Woodpecker	3x3–4x4	8–14	1¼–1½	6–14	6–20	Open woodlands, edges, farms, some urban areas.
Golden-fronted Woodpecker	6x6	12–15	2	9–12	12–20	Deciduous woodlands in Texas and Oklahoma.
Hairy Woodpecker	5x5–6x6	12–16	1½–2¾	9–14	12–20	Forest edges and open woodlands.
Northern Flicker	6x6–8x8	14–24	2–3	10–20	6–20	Open woodlands, fields, meadows, some suburban areas.
Red-bellied Woodpecker	5x5–6x6	12–16	1¾–2¾	10–14	12–20	Deciduous forests.
Red-headed Woodpecker	5x5–6x6	12–16	1¾–2¾	9–14	12–20	Open areas and field edges.
Wrens						
Carolina Wren	4x4–5x5	9–12	1–1½	6–7	6–10	Forests with thick underbrush, backyards near buildings.
Bewick's Wren	4x4–5x5	9–12	1–1½	6–7	6–10	Farms, brushland, suburbs.
House Wren	4x4–5x5	9–12	1–1½	6–7	6–10	Brush edges, backyards.
Other						
House Sparrow	4x4–5x5	8–12	1³⁄₁₆–2	6–8	4–12	Widely distributed: backyards, farms, suburbs, cities.
Starling	5x5–6x6	13–20	1⅝–4	6–16	10–25	Widely distributed: backyards, farms, suburbs, cities.

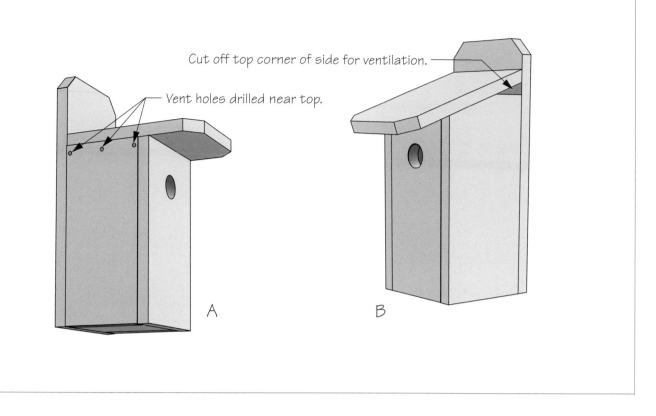

Cut off top corner of side for ventilation.

Vent holes drilled near top.

A

B

Birdhouses need adequate ventilation to guard against overheating. Boring holes near the top or cutting off the upper corner of each side allows for air circulation.

Although there is no consensus on the exact entry diameter for every species of cavity nesters, it's generally understood that a hole 1$\frac{1}{2}$ inches in diameter will exclude starlings but accommodate other small birds. Unfortunately, reducing the hole size will have little impact on House Sparrows—unless the hole is 1$\frac{1}{8}$ inches in diameter. This small sparrow can fit through a 1$\frac{3}{16}$-inch hole.

It might seem to us that a bird needs a perch just below the entry hole. In fact, this is unnecessary and could possibly be an aid for a predator or competitor. Cavity-nesting birds have strong feet and legs and have no trouble perching on the bottom edge of the hole.

CONSTRUCTION NOTES

It isn't necessary to make your birdhouses watertight; some seepage is inevitable. Most nests are built so that the eggs are well above the floor, insulated from accumulated moisture. Good drainage is desirable, however. This is easily provided by drilling a few holes in the floor or lopping off the corners of the floor. Be careful not to drive nails or screws through the drain holes.

Holes in the floor also increase ventilation, necessary in all birdhouses. It's also a good idea to drill a few $\frac{1}{4}$-inch holes, or a single $\frac{1}{2}$-inch hole, on each side near the top, or cut off the top corner of each side.

Often overlooked during construction of birdhouses is a means of quick, easy access for monitoring and cleaning. Adding hinges to the top or pivots to one of the sides will allow you to open the box and peek inside while causing as little disruption to the nestlings as possible. Some of the houses in this book have a front or side panel that pivots outward on two screws or nails. You can also hinge a side panel or roof section with stock hinges purchased at a hardware store. Another alternative is to use a strip of vinyl, rubber (inner tubing, for example), or nylon webbing. Use small screws, nails, or staples to hold the hinges in place. You need to make sure that the hinged panel or roof fastens securely so that predators won't be able to pry it open. Use hooks and eyes, screws, pins, or other fasteners to secure the hinged part.

Even if you don't plan to monitor a nestbox, you'll need a way to open the box to clean it. If you've used screws for some or all of the assembly, removing the roof or a side panel can be done easily with little harm to the structure. A problem with many mass-produced birdhouses is that they are stapled together, making them nearly impossible to get apart without damage. Several of the birdhouse plans presented here include suggestions on how to make the box accessible.

Once the nestlings are ready to fledge, their exit from the house will be easier if you've added footholds for the young birds to use. Simply cut a series of saw kerfs or install a piece of 1/4-inch hardware cloth on the inside below the entrance hole.

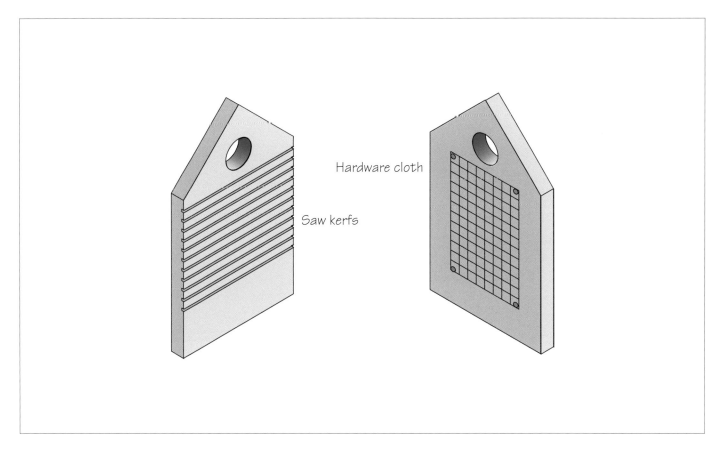

Hardware cloth

Saw kerfs

Saw kerfs or hardware cloth give fledglings a foothold when they're ready to leave the nest.

The easiest birdhouse to make is the simple box house. The first three sets of drawings illustrate variations on the same theme.

FLAT ROOF AND FORWARD-SLOPING ROOF

The dimensions given in the illustrations for the first two houses are suitable for smaller birds. These dimensions, as well as those for all of the nestboxes, can be easily adjusted to suit just about any cavity-nesting bird. See Table 3 under Birdhouse Basics for dimension guidelines.

In the flat roof and forward-sloping roof designs, the back of the simple box house extends upward past the roof. This projection facilitates hanging on the side of a building, a post, or a tree. Just drill a 3/8-inch hole through the projection and hook the box over a nail or screw.

Aside from the roof, these two versions differ in how the sides fit to the front and back. The orientation of the front and sides is arbitrary—either way will work with either model. In the flat-roofed model shown here, the sides fit between the front and back. One side or the other can be hinged on a pair of screws. A third screw secures the door at the bottom. In the version with the forward-sloping roof, the front is cut narrower than the back and fits between the sides. The front hinges in the same manner as the side in the other model.

Birds that will nest in the Simple Box House with a Flat Roof or a Forward-sloping Roof

Bluebirds
Chickadees
Finches
Flycatchers
Titmice
Tree Swallows
Violet-green Swallows
Wrens

Entry diameter: 1¹/₂"
Floor dimensions: 5" × 5"

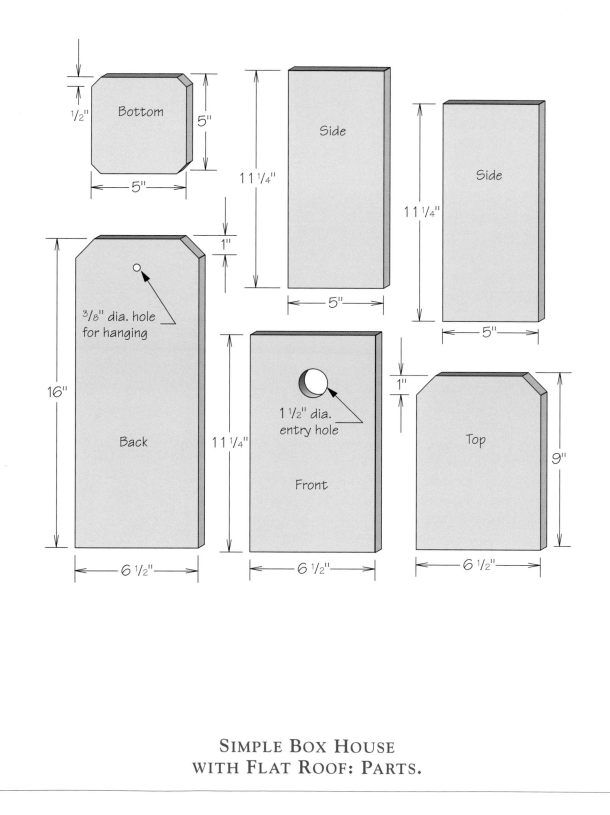

1/2"

Bottom

5"

5"

Side

11 1/4"

5"

Side

11 1/4"

5"

1"

3/8" dia. hole
for hanging

16"

Back

6 1/2"

1 1/2" dia.
entry hole

11 1/4"

Front

6 1/2"

1"

Top

9"

6 1/2"

SIMPLE BOX HOUSE
WITH FLAT ROOF: PARTS.

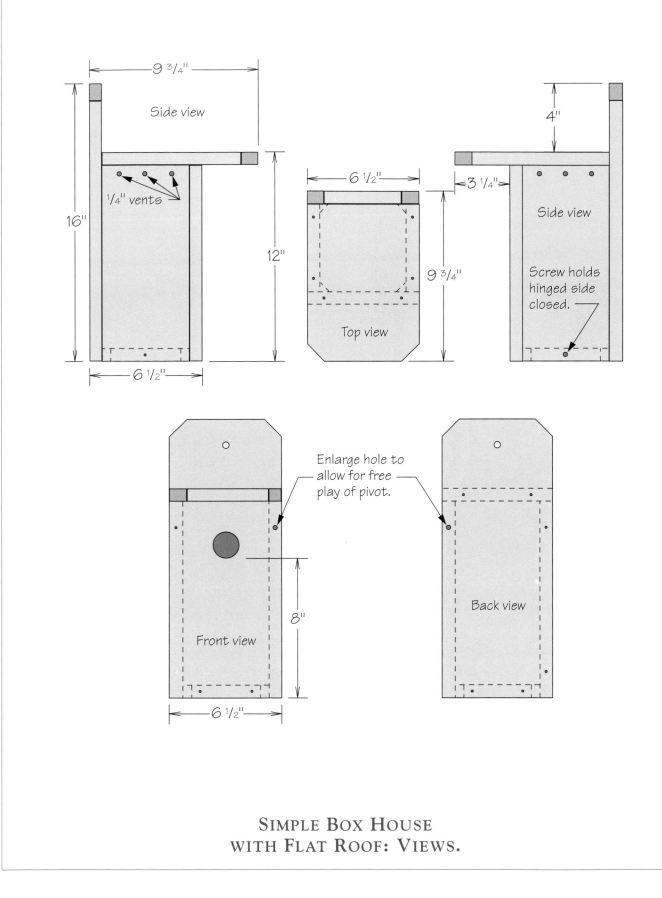

9 ¾"

Side view

¼" vents

16"

6 ½"

12"

6 ½"

Top view

9 ¾"

4"

3 ¼"

Side view

Screw holds
hinged side
closed.

Enlarge hole to
allow for free
play of pivot.

8"

Front view

6 ½"

Back view

**SIMPLE BOX HOUSE
WITH FLAT ROOF: VIEWS.**

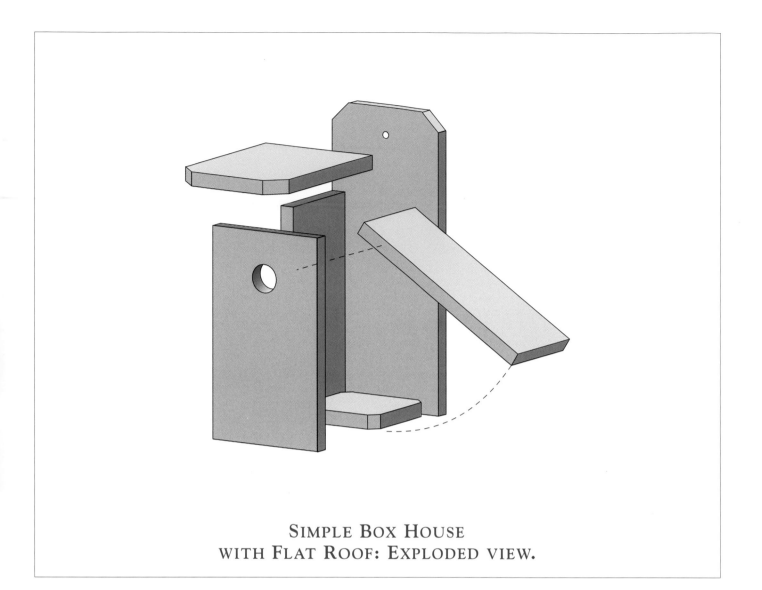

**SIMPLE BOX HOUSE
WITH FLAT ROOF: EXPLODED VIEW.**

CONSTRUCTION NOTES

First study the drawings of the simple box house you want to build. Cut all the pieces to the dimensions shown in the drawings.

For the Flat Roof project, cut all the ends square. Cutting the corners off the top and back is optional. Then cut the corners off the bottom piece for drainage and increased ventilation. Bore two or three $1/4$-inch-diameter holes along the top edge of each side for ventilation. Also bore the $1^1/2$-inch-diameter entry hole about 8 inches from the bottom edge.

Bore an optional $3/8$-inch diameter hole in the back for hanging.

Fasten the bottom to one of the sides with two $1^1/2$-inch screws or 4d galvanized box nails. Drill pilot holes in the sides first so that you don't split the wood.

Next attach the front and the back. Before installing the other side, drill a $1/8$-inch-diameter hole in the front, about $1^1/4$ inches down from the top and $3/8$ inch in from the edge. Drill a corresponding hole in the back. These enlarged holes allow the fastening screws or nails to pivot so that the side can be opened. When installing the sides, don't drive the screws or nails tight. To get a loose fit, it might be necessary to rip or plane this side a little narrower than the other. You might also need to round the upper edge of the side so that it doesn't catch on the roof as it swings open.

With the side in place loosely, fasten the top using screws or nails driven through the top and into the front and fixed side. Also, drive two screws or nails through the back into the top. Finally, use a screw at the bottom of the hinged side to hold it closed.

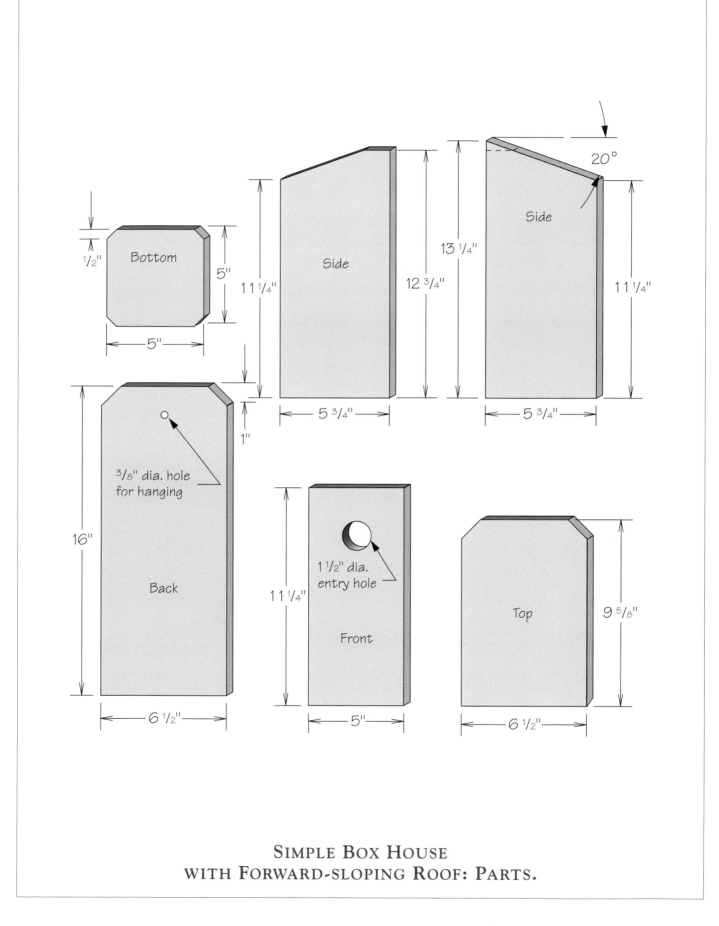

**SIMPLE BOX HOUSE
WITH FORWARD-SLOPING ROOF: PARTS.**

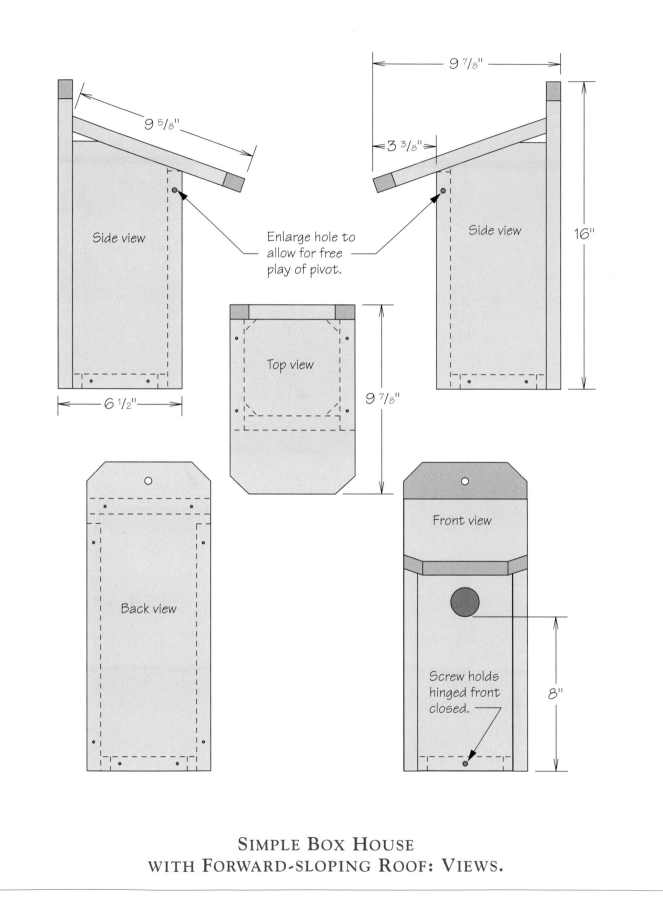

9 7/8"

9 5/8"

3 3/8"

16"

Side view

Side view

Enlarge hole to
allow for free
play of pivot.

Top view

9 7/8"

6 1/2"

Back view

Front view

Screw holds
hinged front
closed.

8"

SIMPLE BOX HOUSE
WITH FORWARD-SLOPING ROOF: VIEWS.

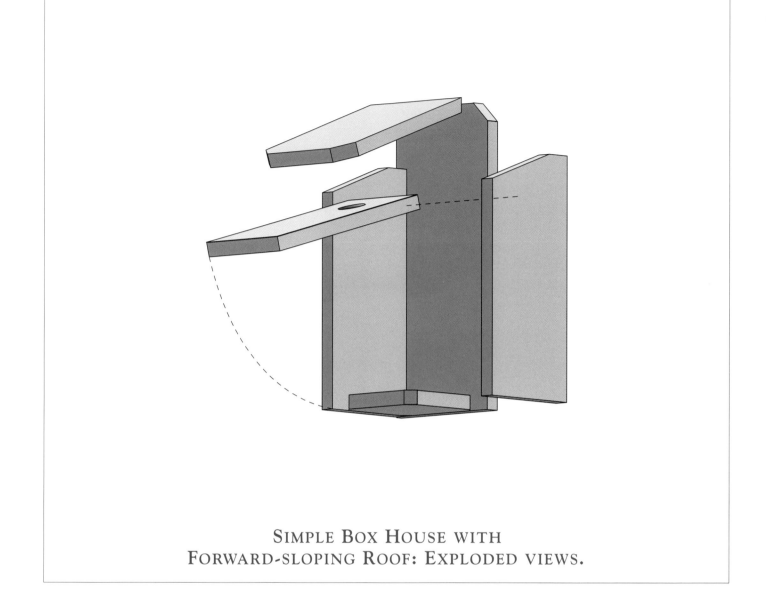

**SIMPLE BOX HOUSE WITH
FORWARD-SLOPING ROOF: EXPLODED VIEWS.**

For the Forward-sloping Roof project, cut the angle on each side, then cut off the upper corner for ventilation. Cut the corners off the bottom, also for ventilation and drainage.

Cutting the corners off the back and top is optional, but you will need to cut a 20-degree bevel along the upper edge of the top where it meets the back. Drill a $1^{1}/_{2}$-inch-diameter entry hole in the front, approximately 8 inches from the bottom edge, and an optional $^{3}/_{8}$-inch-diameter hole in the back for hanging.

Before assembling the pieces, drill a $^{1}/_{8}$-inch-diameter hole in each side for the pivoting front panel. Locate these holes about $1^{1}/_{4}$ inches down and $^{3}/_{8}$ inch in from the edge.

Begin the assembly by mounting the side pieces to the bottom with $1^{1}/_{2}$-inch screws or 4d galvanized box nails. Drill pilot holes to prevent splitting the wood. Then fasten the back to the sides and bottom.

Put the top onto the assembly and drive two screws or nails through the back into the back edge of the top. Drive them at a slight angle so they don't poke through. Next, while making sure that the sides of the birdhouse are flush with the sides of the roof piece, fasten the roof to the sides. Check the fit of the front between the sides. If it doesn't fit loosely, plane the edges. Drive a screw or a nail through each of the enlarged holes in the sides. The front should pivot easily. Drive a single screw at the bottom of the front to hold the front closed.

REVERSE-SLOPING ROOF

This simple box birdhouse is similar in construction to the previous two, but it's a bit larger to accommodate some of the bigger birds. As with the other houses, you can vary the dimensions to suit a particular species. The drawings show a 2-inch entry, but depending on the bird you're building for, you might need to make a larger entry hole.

CONSTRUCTION NOTES

Cut out all the parts for the Simple Box House. Cut the sides and back with a 10-degree angle to give the slope to the roof. Cut the corners off the floor for ventilation and drainage. Bore two $^1/_8$-inch-diameter holes in the upper corner of each side, about $1^1/_2$ inches down from the top and $^3/_8$ inch in from the front edges. Notice that the pivoting front is cut $^1/_4$ inch shorter than the long edges of the side. This clearance allows for the free swing of the front when opening it and also gives additional ventilation. Cut the entry hole in the front.

To begin assembly, use two $1^1/_4$-inch screws or 3d galvanized box nails to fasten the sides to the back. Drill pilot holes to prevent splitting the wood. Next, fit the bottom into place and secure it with two $1^1/_2$-inch screws or 4d galvanized nails driven through both sides and the back.

Now put on the top, fastening it with five or six screws or nails. Make sure the sides are flush with the edges of the top.

Check the fit of the front to see how well it fits between the sides. If it's too tight, plane or rip it down for an easy fit. While holding the front flush with the bottom, drive two screws through the pivot holes into the front. Don't drive them too tightly. Fasten the front at the bottom with a single screw.

Birds that will nest in the Simple Box House with a Reverse-sloping Roof

Kestrels
Saw-whet Owls
Woodpeckers

Entry diameter: 2" to 3"
Floor dimenstions: 6" × 6" 8" × 8"

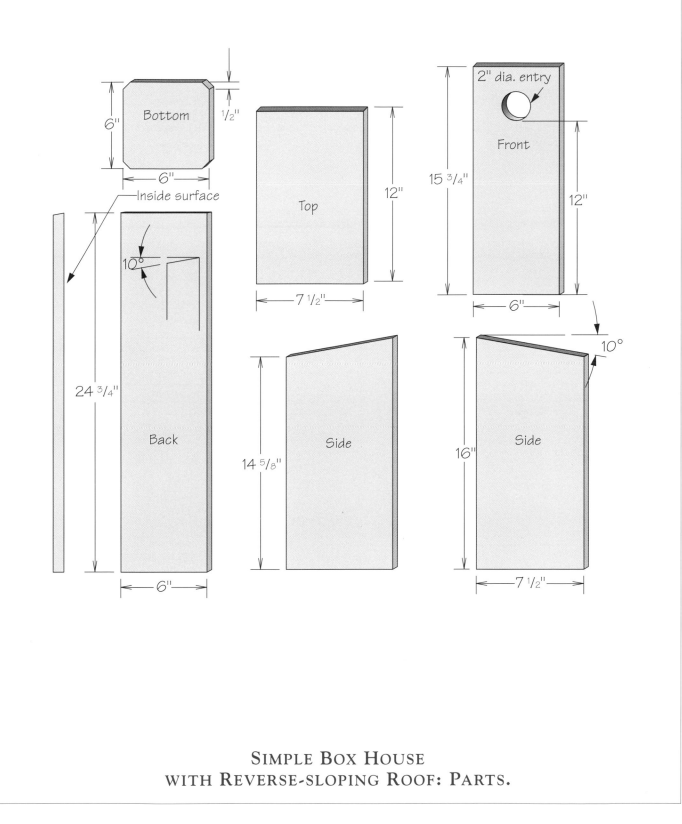

**SIMPLE BOX HOUSE
WITH REVERSE-SLOPING ROOF: PARTS.**

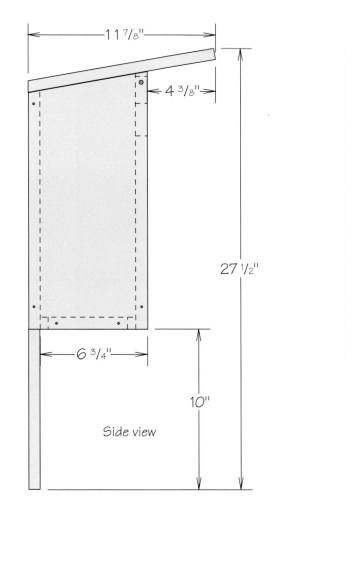

11 7/8"

4 3/8"

27 1/2"

6 3/4"

10"

Side view

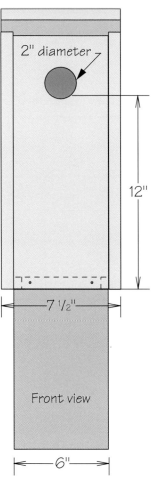

2" diameter

12"

7 1/2"

Front view

6"

SIMPLE BOX HOUSE
WITH REVERSE-SLOPING ROOF: VIEWS.

SIMPLE BOX HOUSE WITH
REVERSE-SLOPING ROOF: EXPLODED VIEW.

GABLE HOUSE

The gable house, made to the same dimensions as the first two simple box houses, will attract the same set of birds. The front and back are cut at 45-degree angles. Because the roof forms a 90-degree angle, no special cuts are needed to join the two roof segments. The back can be extended below the floor for mounting to a wooden post or other flat surface. Use two screws horizontally or vertically to hold the box securely. Alternatively, you can cut the back the same length as the front and then bottom mount the box or hang it with a cord strung through a pair of screw eyes driven into the top.

With the roof extending beyond the back, you can't easily mount the house on the side of a building or tree trunk. If you wish to do so, it's a simple matter to move the roof forward to make it flush with the back.

If you don't plan on suspending this house with wire or cord, you can hinge the roof, as shown in the exploded view. Use stock hinges or a strip of rubber or vinyl fastened along the ridge. You can hinge one of the sides, but be careful when opening it once there are eggs or nestlings inside; if the nest is built high off the floor, the top of the hinged door could damage the nest or harm the birds.

CONSTRUCTION NOTES

Cut out all the parts. If you've extended the back (as shown in the illustrations), line up the front to the back and make sure the roof angles match. With both pieces together, use the bottom edge of the front as a guide to transfer a line to the back as a reference to help locate the floor.

Fasten each side to the floor with two $1^1/2$-inch screws or 4d galvanized box nails. Drill pilot holes to prevent splitting the wood. Then fasten the front to the assembly. Make sure you keep the sides flush with the edges of the front. Place the assembly face down on the bench and fasten the back into place, checking to make sure the bottom is along the reference line.

Now assemble the roof with either two screws or nails or with hinges. If hinged, fasten the roof with four screws or nails on the fixed side only. Secure the hinged side with a hook and eye.

Birds that will nest in the Gable House

Bluebirds

Chickadees

Finches

Flycatchers

Titmice

Tree Swallows

Violet-green Swallows

Wrens

Entry diameter: $1^1/2$"

Floor dimensions: 5" × 5"

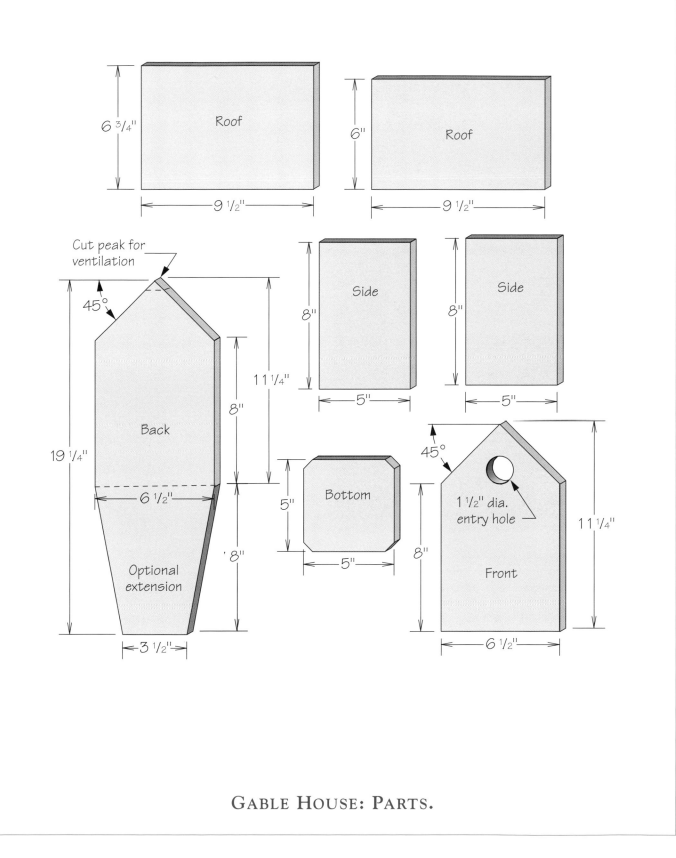

6 3/4" Roof **9 1/2"**

6" Roof **9 1/2"**

Cut peak for ventilation

45°

Back

Side **8"** **5"**

Side **8"** **5"**

11 1/4"

8"

19 1/4"

6 1/2"

Optional extension

8"

3 1/2"

5" Bottom **5"**

8"

45°

1 1/2" dia. entry hole

11 1/4"

Front

6 1/2"

Gable House: Parts.

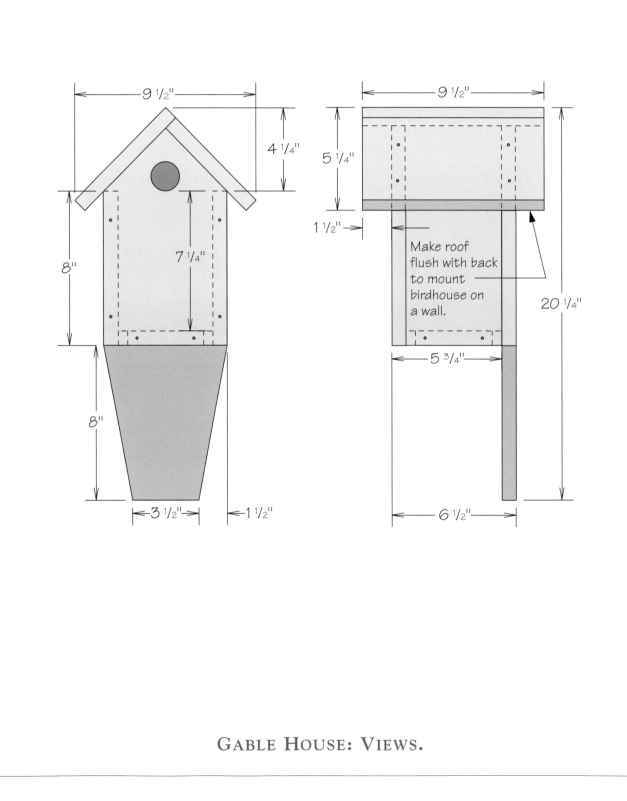

9 1/2"

4 1/4"

7 1/4"

8"

8"

3 1/2"

1 1/2"

9 1/2"

5 1/4"

1 1/2"

Make roof
flush with back
to mount
birdhouse on
a wall.

20 1/4"

5 3/4"

6 1/2"

GABLE HOUSE: VIEWS.

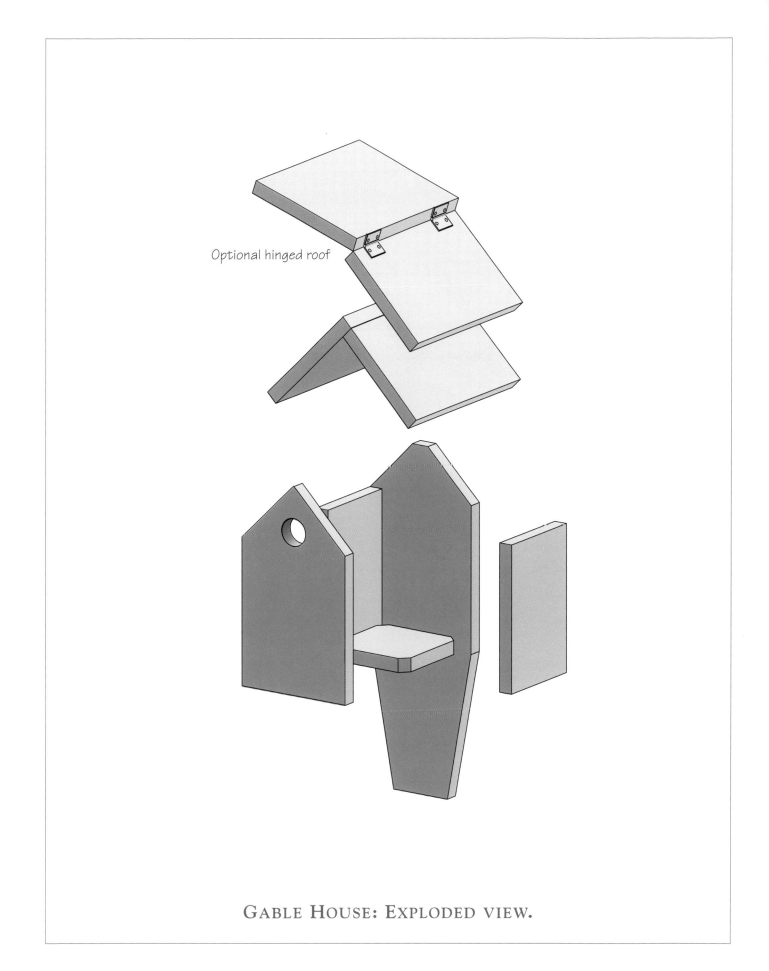

Optional hinged roof

GABLE HOUSE: EXPLODED VIEW.

WREN CUBE

The traditional wren house may also be used by some of the other small birds. Its design suggests that it be kept small, but it can't be too small—there must be at least $5^1/2$ inches between the floor and the bottom of the entry hole. This house looks terrific hung among branches, but it can be mounted on a post or wall as well.

CONSTRUCTION NOTES

Cut out all the parts according to the dimensions shown in the illustration. Cut the $1^1/2$-inch-diameter entry hole $6^3/4$ inches from the bottom corner of the front. Make a few saw kerfs in the larger of the two side pieces for drainage and ventilation. Alternatively, you can drill three or four $1/4$-inch-diameter holes up through the assembled pieces.

Use two $1^1/2$-inch screws or 4d galvanized box nails to fasten the two bottom/side pieces together. Drill pilot holes to prevent splitting the wood. Then fasten the front and back. Put the roof together in the same way as the sides, then mount the roof to the assembly with screws so that it can be removed for cleaning

Birds that will nest in the Wren Cube

Wrens
Chickadees
Titmice
Tree Swallows
Violet-green Swallows

Entry diameter: $1^1/2$"

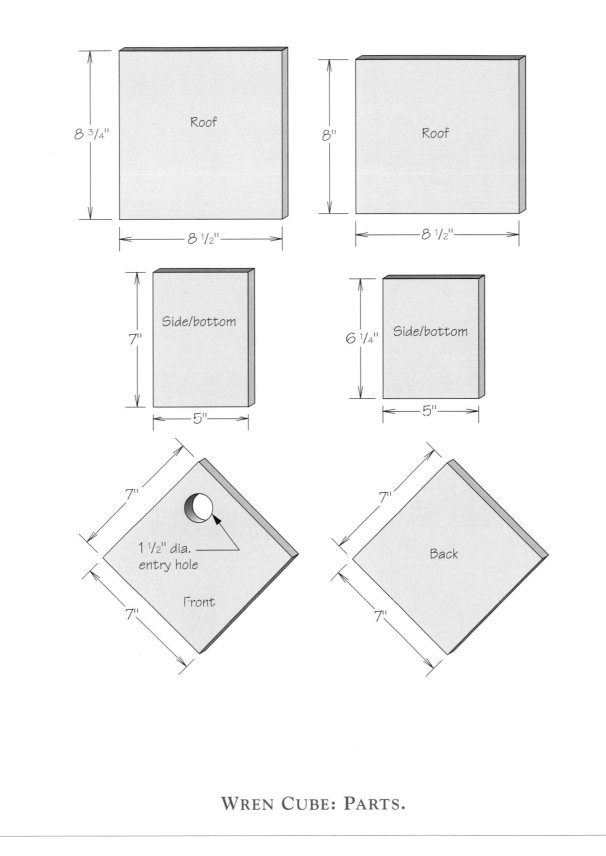

WREN CUBE: PARTS.

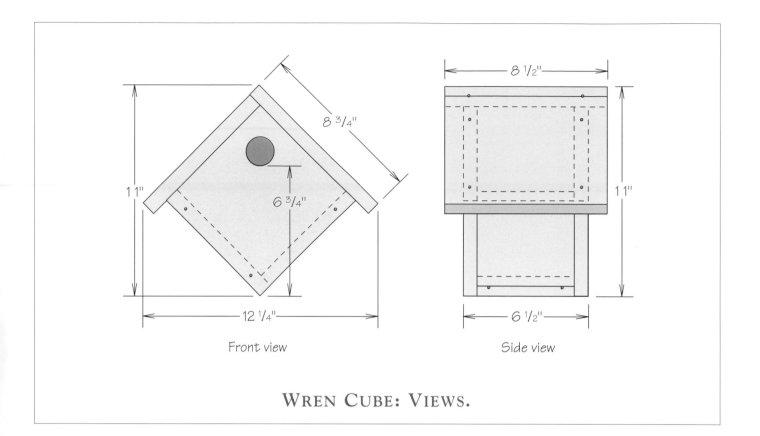

Front view

Side view

WREN CUBE: VIEWS.

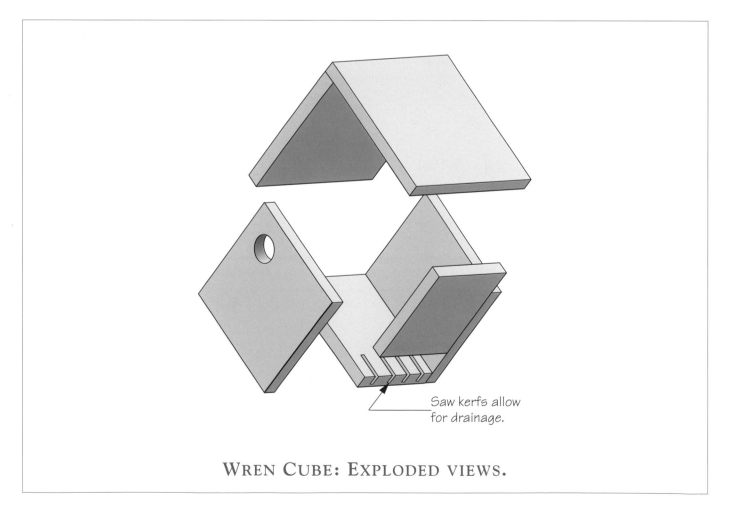

Saw kerfs allow
for drainage.

WREN CUBE: EXPLODED VIEWS.

CHALET

The chalet has a few more angles to it than the other models, so it's a bit more difficult to build. Not only do the sides flare outward from the bottom, the gabled roof flares outward at the ridge. Like the wren house, it should be kept small.

CONSTRUCTION NOTES

After examining the drawings, cut out the parts according to the dimensions shown in the illustration. Pay particular attention to the bevels on the bottom and at the ridge. If you make the bottom too small, it will fall through. It's better to cut it a bit larger so that it will wedge itself into place. Lop off the corners of the floor for ventilation and drainage.

Begin assembling the chalet by attaching the front and back to the sides with two $1^1/2$-inch screws or 4d galvanized nails in each joint. Drill pilot holes to prevent splitting the wood. Drop the floor into place. A single screw or nail driven through each side is sufficient to hold it.

Attach the roof to the assembly with four screws driven through each roof panel.

Birds that will nest in the Chalet

House Finches
Barn Swallows
Prothonotary Warblers
Violet-green Swallows

Entry diameter: $1^1/2$"
Floor dimensions: 4" × 4"

35

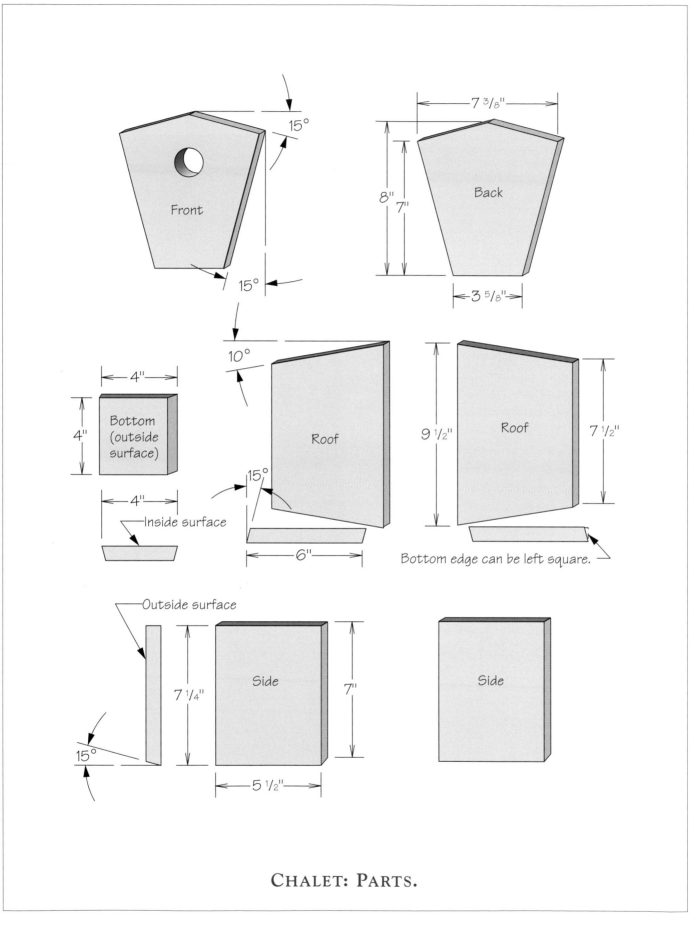

15°

7 3/8"

8"
7"

Back

3 5/8"

4"

4"

Bottom
(outside
surface)

10°

4"

Inside surface

Front

15°

15°

15°

Roof

6"

9 1/2"

Roof

7 1/2"

Bottom edge can be left square.

Outside surface

7 1/4"

Side

7"

Side

5 1/2"

15°

CHALET: PARTS.

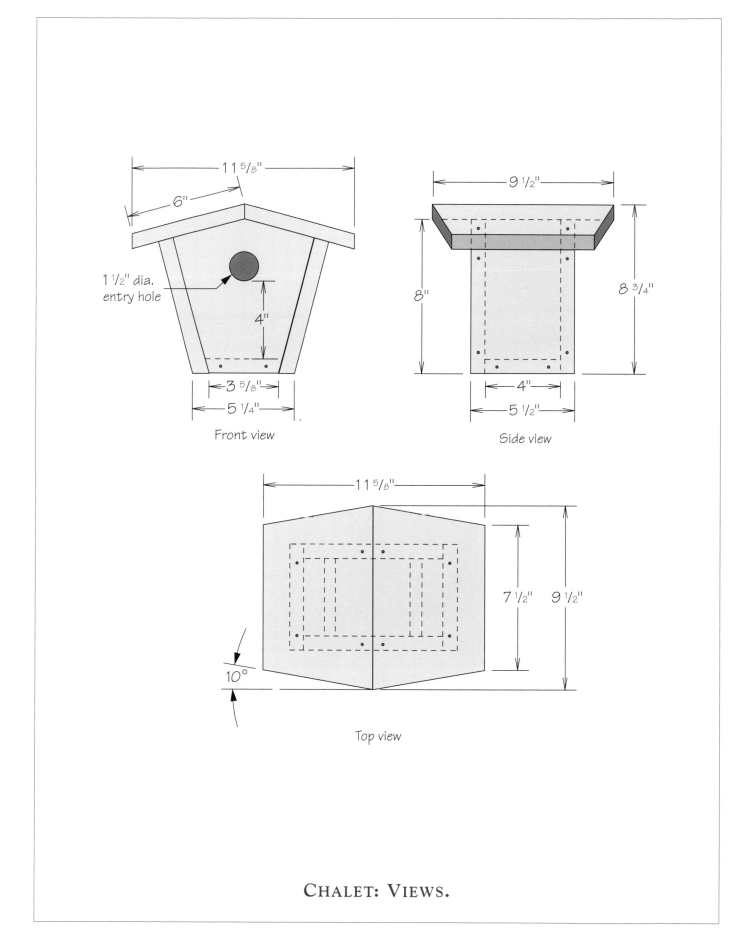

1 1/2" dia.
entry hole

Front view

Side view

Top view

CHALET: VIEWS.

CHALET: EXPLODED VIEW.

PETERSON BLUEBIRD HOUSE

The Peterson house was designed especially for bluebirds. If bluebirds aren't in your area, yet you like the design, by all means build the Peterson anyway—the box is suitable for many of the smaller birds.

CONSTRUCTION NOTES

Cut out the parts according to the dimensions shown in the illustration. The side pieces determine the angles of the front and top. The top, front, bottom, and back each have a 25-degree-angle cut on one end. Cut the 1^1/$_2$-inch-diameter entry hole about eight inches from the bottom. Use a rasp to level out the bottom of the hole.

To assemble, attach the sides to the back, keeping the top and back edges flush. Use two 1^1/$_2$-inch screws or 4d galvanized box nails in each joint. Drill pilot holes first so that you don't split the wood. Fit the front between the sides and fasten with two or three nails or screws. If this piece is cut too narrow it will fall through. Make it a little wider if necessary.

Fasten the top with four screws to make it easily removable for cleaning.

Birds that will nest in the Peterson Bluebird House

Bluebirds
Chickadees
Finches
Flycatchers
Titmice
Tree Swallows
Violet-green Swallows
Wrens

Entry diameter: 1^1/$_2$"
Floor dimensions: 2 ^{3}/$_8$" × 5"

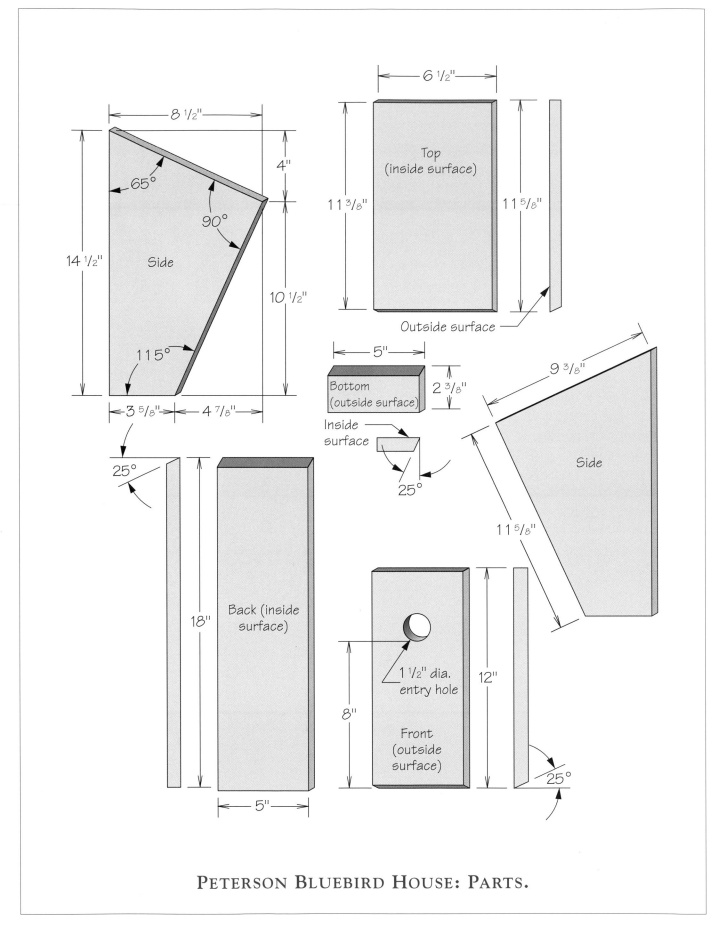

8 1/2"

65°

90°

14 1/2"

Side

4"

10 1/2"

115°

3 5/8"   4 7/8"

6 1/2"

Top
(inside surface)

11 3/8"

11 5/8"

Outside surface

5"

Bottom
(outside surface)

2 3/8"

Inside
surface

25°

9 3/8"

Side

11 5/8"

25°

18"

Back (inside
surface)

1 1/2" dia.
entry hole

12"

8"

Front
(outside
surface)

25°

5"

PETERSON BLUEBIRD HOUSE: PARTS.

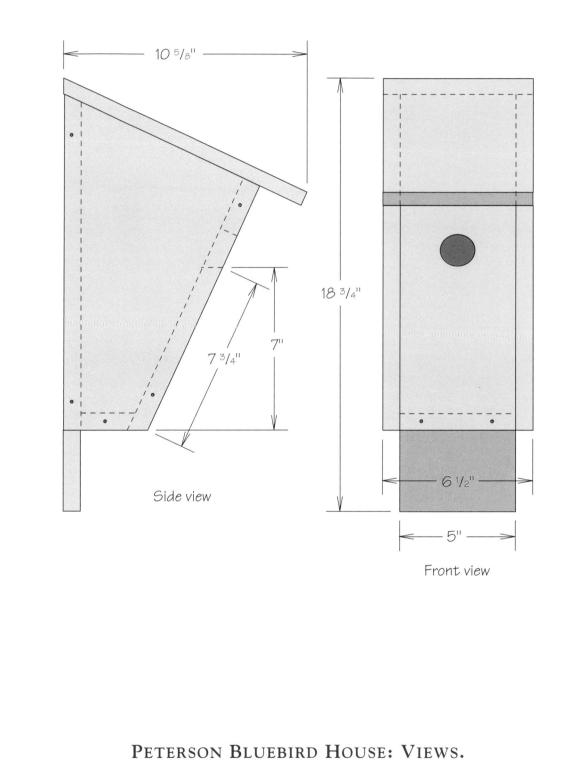

10 ⁵/₈"

18 ³/₄"

7"

7 ³/₄"

6 ¹/₂"

5"

Side view

Front view

PETERSON BLUEBIRD HOUSE: VIEWS.

PETERSON BLUEBIRD HOUSE:
EXPLODED VIEW.

LARGE HOUSE FOR DUCKS AND OWLS

Larger birds need larger houses. All the other birdhouses described are dimensioned using $^3/_4$-inch stock; this larger house is drawn using $^1/_2$-inch plywood. It can also be built with $^5/_8$-inch or $^3/_4$-inch stock.

CONSTRUCTION NOTES

Cut out all of the parts according to the dimensions shown in the illustration. Cut an entry hole in the front appropriate for the birds you hope to attract. (See Table 3 on pages 12 and 13.)

Locate the positions of the two cleats on the inside surfaces of the front and back and use three $1^1/_4$-inch screws or 3d galvanized box nails to fasten the cleats. Then fasten each side to the front and back, using four or five screws or nails in each joint. Drill pilot holes first.

Drill four $^1/_4$-inch-diameter ventilation and drainage holes in the bottom 1 inch in from each corner. Drop the bottom into place. Secure the bottom with a screw driven through the front, back, and sides. This makes it easy to remove the bottom for cleaning.

Lay the box on its back and hold the top in place. Trace the outside of the box on the underside of the top. Using these marks as guides, fasten cleats to the underside of the top with three screws or nails. Use hooks and eyes to hold the top firmly in place.

Ducks and owls that will nest in the Large House

Ducks:
Barrow's Goldeneyes
Common Goldeneyes
Common Mergansers
Hooded Mergansers
Wood Ducks
Owls:
Barn Owls
Barred Owls
Eastern Screech Owls
Northern Saw-whet Owls
Western Screech Owls

Entry diameter: 2" to 5"
Floor dimensions: 12" × 12"

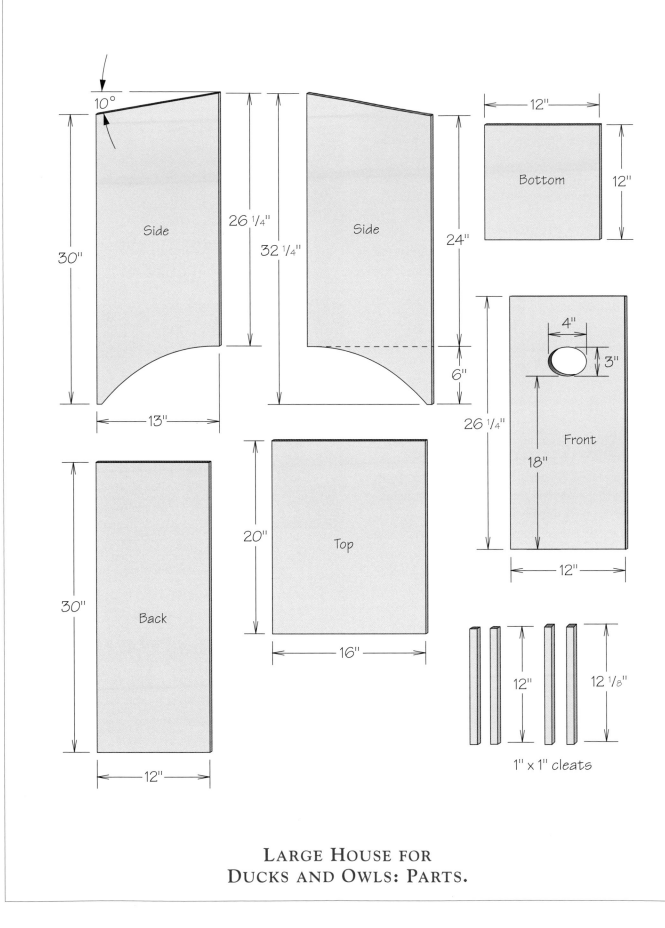

**LARGE HOUSE FOR
DUCKS AND OWLS: PARTS.**

Side

Side

Bottom
12"
12"

10°

30"
26 1/4"
32 1/4"

24"

13"

6"

4"
3"

Front
26 1/4"
18"

12"

Back
30"

20"
Top

16"

12"

12"
12 1/8"

1" x 1" cleats

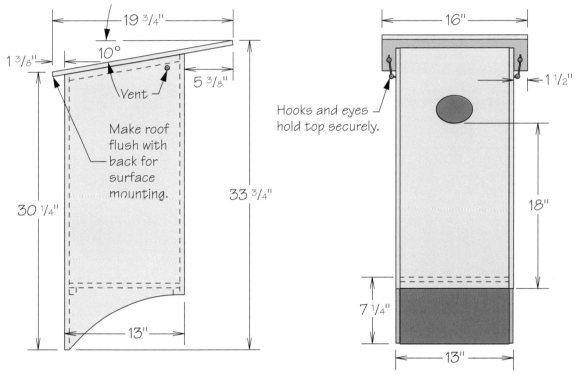

19 ³/₄"

10°

1 ³/₈"

Vent

5 ³/₈"

Make roof
flush with
back for
surface
mounting.

30 ¹/₄"

33 ³/₄"

13"

Side view

16"

Hooks and eyes
hold top securely.

1 ¹/₂"

18"

7 ¹/₄"

13"

Front view

**LARGE HOUSE FOR
DUCKS AND OWLS: VIEWS.**

Cleats fastened to removable top hold it in place.

**LARGE HOUSE FOR
DUCKS AND OWLS: EXPLODED VIEW.**

HEXAGONAL HOUSE

Building this house is a little more challenging. It requires that the edges of each of the six side segments be ripped at a 30-degree angle. For best results, use wood that is thoroughly dry; otherwise the joints will tend to open as the wood dries.

The back segment is elongated for mounting on a tree trunk, post, or wall. If you'd rather suspend the hexagonal house, cut the back the same length as the other sides; put an eye bolt in the center of the top, and hang the house from a wire or cord.

CONSTRUCTION NOTES

To begin, rip the side segments with the 30-degree angles, then cut them to length.

The top retainer fits into a rabbet cut made in the top of the segments, and dado cuts hold the bottom. I recommend using 3/4-inch or 1/2-inch exterior plywood for the retainer and the bottom, because there is no chance of the plywood splitting. Cut the rabbets and dadoes to fit the material you use. If you make the back segment longer than the others, be sure to cut the dado in the same place relative to the other pieces. Bore the entry hole in the front segment.

Now make the top retainer and the bottom pieces. The exact size of each hexagon will depend on the depth of the dadoes and rabbets. A little trial and error might be necessary. It's okay if these pieces are slightly smaller than the actual shape formed by the assembled segments. Use a hole saw or a jig saw to cut a hole in the top retainer.

Use a band clamp or heavy rubber bands to hold the segments together around the retainer and the bottom while securing them with 1-inch screws or 3d galvanized box nails driven to the face of each segment.

Next, drill three 1/4-inch-diameter holes through the bottom for drainage. Also drill a 1/4-inch-diameter hole in the center of each of the four side segments, just below the retainer, for ventilation.

Finally cut the top and secure it to the top retainer with four 1-inch screws. The top is easily removable, and the hole in the retainer allows for cleaning without having to disassemble any of the segments.

Birds that will nest in the Hexagonal House

Ash-throated Flycatchers
Hairy Woodpeckers
Golden-fronted Woodpeckers
Great Crested Flycatchers
Northern Flickers
Red-bellied Woodpeckers
Red-headed Woodpeckers

Entry diameter: 2" to 2 1/2"
Floor dimensions: 5 3/8" × 5 3/8"

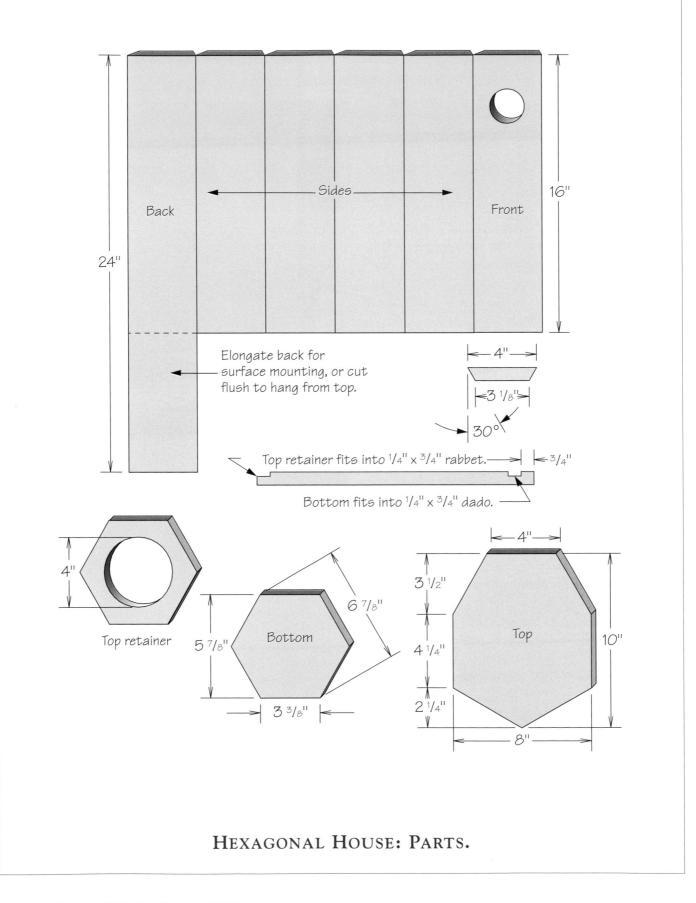

Back

Sides

Front

24"

16"

Elongate back for surface mounting, or cut flush to hang from top.

4"

3 1/8"

30°

Top retainer fits into 1/4" x 3/4" rabbet.

3/4"

Bottom fits into 1/4" x 3/4" dado.

Top retainer

4"

Bottom

5 7/8"

6 7/8"

3 3/8"

Top

4"

3 1/2"

4 1/4"

2 1/4"

10"

8"

HEXAGONAL HOUSE: PARTS.

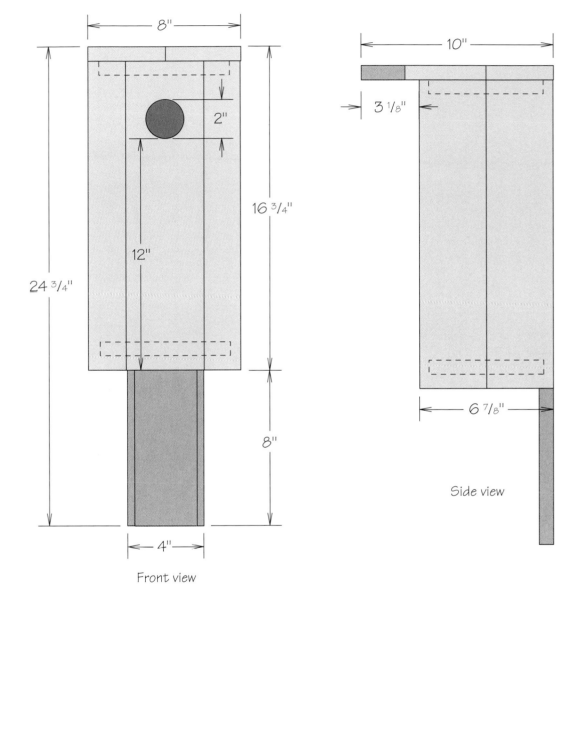

8"

2"

16 3/4"

12"

24 3/4"

10"

3 1/8"

8"

6 7/8"

4"

Front view

Side view

HEXAGONAL HOUSE: VIEWS.

HEXAGONAL HOUSE: EXPLODED VIEW.

PURPLE MARTIN HIGH-RISE

Most cavity-nesting birds are territorial, and only one nesting pair will use a given area. Not so with the communal Purple Martins.

Here's an original design of a high-rise dwelling for twelve nesting pairs of Purple Martins. It might look complicated at first glance, but it's really quite simple because it's made of four identical three-story units. The front panel of each unit pivots open at the top for cleaning and is secured at the bottom with a screw driven through one or both sides or with a hook and eye.

CONSTRUCTION NOTES

Begin by cutting out the parts according to the dimensions shown in the illustration. Remember, all four units will require four times as many pieces.

Bore the 2-inch-diameter entry holes in the front panels. Cut the 25-degree angles on the upper end of the back and along the ridge of each roof. You can leave the bottom edges of the roof pieces square. Bore a $1/2$-inch-diameter hole in the upper corner of each side. Also bore a $1/8$-inch-diameter hole in each side about $1^1/4$ inches down and $3/8$ inch in from the edge for the pivoting front panel.

Match each side with its back and lay them on the bench with the insides up and flush at the bottoms. Lay out the floors, marking each position with a pencil.

Fasten the sides to the back with four $1^1/2$-inch screws or 4d galvanized box nails at each joint. Put the floors in next, aligning them with your layout marks, securing each with two screws or nails driven through each side.

Check the fit of the front panel between the sides. It should fit loosely. If it's too tight, plane or rip it down. Now mount the ledges with two screws each driven through the inside face of the front. Put the front panel back into place and drive a screw through each of the pivot holes. Check the swing of the door.

Mount the roof with four screws.

For Purple Martins only.

Entry diameter: 2"
Floor dimensions: 6" × 6"

To assemble the four units, first join two of them back to back with four $1^3/8$-inch screws driven through the inside. Center the remaining two units on each side of the assembly, just below the roof, and attach them in the same manner.

The complete assembly is massive. Mount it solidly atop a sturdy post 10 to 20 feet above the ground.

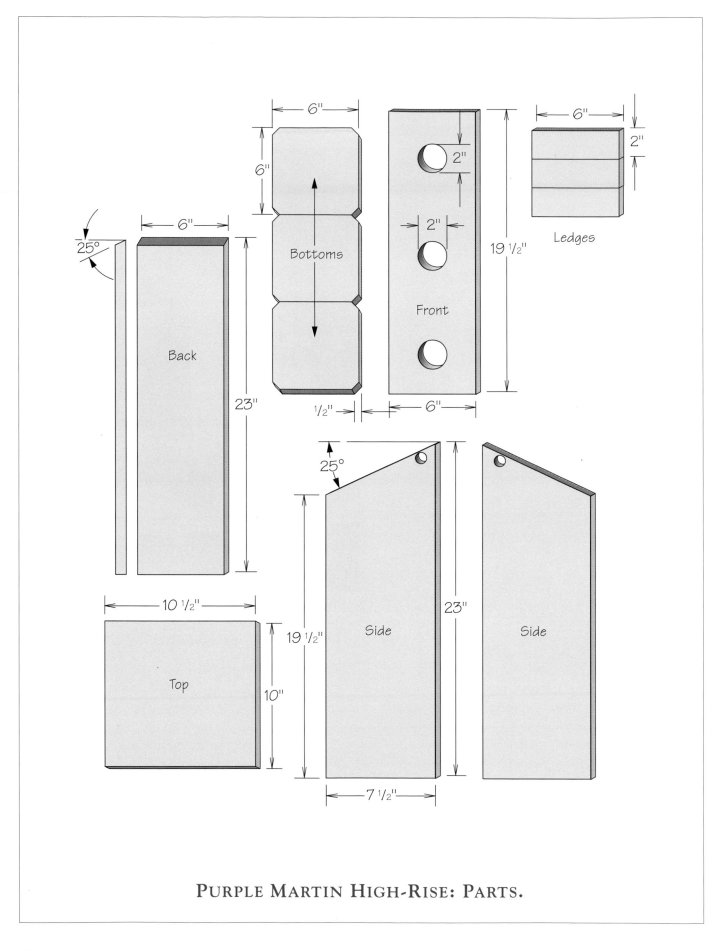

PURPLE MARTIN HIGH-RISE: PARTS.

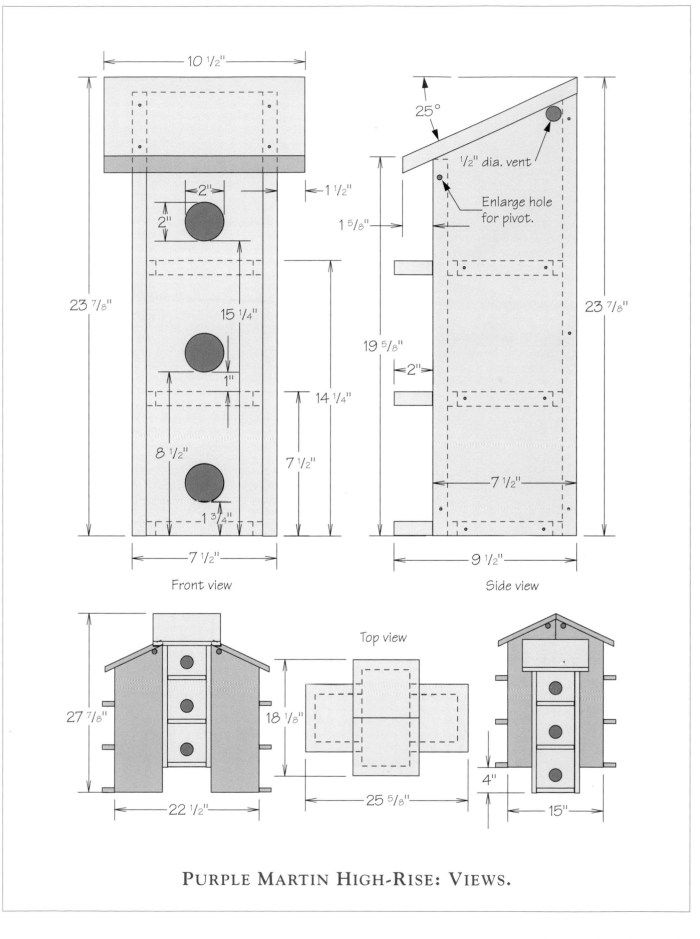

10 1/2"

2"

2"

1 1/2"

23 7/8"

15 1/4"

1"

14 1/4"

8 1/2"

7 1/2"

1 3/4"

7 1/2"

Front view

25°

1/2" dia. vent

Enlarge hole for pivot.

1 5/8"

19 5/8"

2"

23 7/8"

7 1/2"

9 1/2"

Side view

Top view

27 7/8"

18 1/8"

4"

22 1/2"

25 5/8"

15"

PURPLE MARTIN HIGH-RISE: VIEWS.

PURPLE MARTIN HIGH-RISE:
EXPLODED VIEW.

PLATFORMS

Platform nesters such as American Robins and some phoebes and swallows may use a nesting platform you provide. The illustration (top left and right) shows two types of nesting platforms that are open on three sides. These should be hung out of the weather in a fairly well sheltered area, such as under an eave. Alternatively, the simple box house (bottom) can be modified into a platform enclosed on three sides.

The Black, Say's, and Eastern Phoebes and the Barn and Cliff Swallows can use a platform of about 6 inches square. The platform for the American Robin should be about 8 inches square.

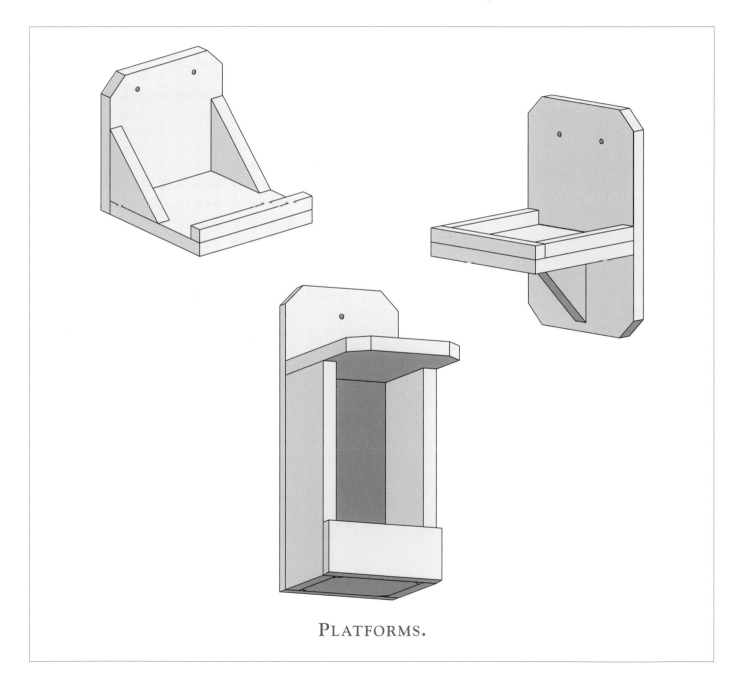

PLATFORMS.

55

BIRD FEEDER BASICS

A bird's life has one focus: survival. Survival involves two main factors: a constant search for food and an overpowering instinct for procreation. By providing birdhouses and feeders, we can help make a bird's life easier. This is especially true in extreme conditions of drought and frost and in newly developed areas where the habitat has been altered and has not yet had a chance to reestablish itself.

We take great satisfaction in knowing that we are helping birds with our efforts, as well as from watching the birds as they come to our yards to feed and to brood their young.

MATERIALS

Building bird feeders is just as easy as building birdhouses. For the most part, materials and techniques are the same. You can use acrylic plastic in hopper-type feeders so that you can see when the seed supply needs to be replenished. Acrylic is readily available, easy to work with, and safe to use. You can cut it with a table saw or scoring knife. If you wish, you can use glass, but working with acrylic plastic is easier and safer. Other materials include hardware cloth and screen, sometimes used for flooring or other applications.

FOOD

Although we say that someone who doesn't eat much eats like a bird, birds are in fact voracious eaters with high energy demands. This is especially so during nesting season and severe cold.

It used to be widely believed that once you put out food at the beginning of winter, you must continue the practice consistently until spring, lest the birds that use your feeders starve. Contemporary thinking, however, holds that this is true only in the severest of situations. Birds gather food from a variety of sources, of which your feeding station is just one. Birds in a given area usually don't depend solely on the kindness of humans to keep them well fed; most birds will simply go elsewhere to find a natural food source.

Another old theory was that if you put out food in the spring, it would encourage migrating birds to stick around instead of flying north. Though it's true that birds will find food where they can and will leave a given area if there is none, migration is instinctive, and birds will leave when their internal clocks tell them it's time. Nevertheless, a good portion of high-protein food from your feeder will serve migrating birds well on their long journey.

So just what should you put out for birds to eat? Collectively, birds will eat just about anything edible. Most bird feeders, however, are designed to hold seeds.

Seed

Seeds are plentiful in the wild. They come from trees, flowers, grasses, and weeds. If you need an excuse not to mow the lawn or weed the garden, you can always say you're building a viable bird habitat. Your neighbors might not appreciate this if you take it to the extreme, however.

Some birds will eat just about any kind of seed; others are picky. To some extent, you can attract certain species to different feeders by being judicious in the seed you put out.

The novice feeder of birds might be tempted to grab a 5-pound package of mixed seed from the pet aisle at

TABLE 4
COMMERCIAL SEED PREFERENCES

SCALE OF 1-2-3, WITH 1 THE MOST PREFERABLE AND 3 SATISFACTORY

Bird	Thistle (Niger)	Striped Sunflower	Black oil Sunflower	Hulled Sunflower	Peanut Kernels*	Millet	Finely Cracked Corn
American Goldfinch	1	2	1	1	-	-	-
Blue Jay	-	2	2	2	1	-	-
Carolina Wren	-	-	-	3	3	3	-
Chickadees (Black-capped, Carolina)	-	2	1	-	3	-	-
Common Grackle	-	2	2	2	3	-	3
Common Redpoll	2	-	-	2	-	3	-
Dark-eyed Junco	3	-	-	2	-	2	3
Grosbeaks (Rose-breasted, Evening)	-	2	1	3	-	-	-
House Finch	2	2	1	1	3	-	-
House Sparrow	-	3	3	3	-	2	3
Mourning Dove	3	3	2	3	-	2	3
Northern Cardinal	-	2	1	3	3	3	3
Nuthatches (White-, Red-breasted)	-	2	2	2	3	-	-
Pine Siskin	2	-	2	-	3	3	-
Purple Finch	3	2	1	3	-	-	-
Red Crossbill	-	2	2	-	-	-	-
Red-winged Blackbird	-	-	-	2	-	2	2
Rufous-Sided Towhee	-	-	-	3	-	2	3
Sparrow (Field)	-	-	-	3	-	2	3
Sparrow (Song, Tree, White-crowned)	3	-	-	3	-	2	3
Sparrow (White-throated)	-	2	2	2	1	2	3
Starling	-	-	-	3	-	-	3
Tufted Titmouse	-	2	2	2	1	-	-
Woodpeckers (Downy, Hairy, Red-bellied)	-	-	3	-	3	-	-

*During nestling season, kernels should be crushed so as not to choke baby birds.

the supermarket while picking up pork chops for dinner. Pound for pound, this isn't such a good buy. Chances are the mix will have few seeds that birds prefer. The rest will get scattered about on the ground, where you'll soon get a crop of who knows what.

It's a good bet to purchase seed at specialty bird shops and pet stores, but expect to pay premium prices. Check out farm co-ops, feed stores, and other seed suppliers for better deals. It's always a good idea to buy in bulk, once you know what your birds are looking for.

You can put out a prepackaged seed mix, but some seeds may be passed up in favor of others. Specialty shops might have mixes made especially for your locale. Consider experimenting with small quantities of various kinds of seeds in different feeders to see which birds are attracted to each. The seed table gives a good idea of what birds enjoy which seeds. Regardless of what kinds of seed you provide, however, range and habitat are the major determining factors of what birds you'll see at your feeders.

Suet, Kitchen Scraps, and Other Foods

Technically, suet is the hard, fatty tissue that surrounds the kidneys of beef and other livestock. It has a traditional use in cooking and tallow making. But for birders, suet can be the renderings of any fat, either commercially prepared or cooked up in your own kitchen.

Birds that like suet include the jays, Brown Creeper, Carolina Wren, chickadees, mockingbird, nuthatches, starling, Tufted Titmouse, Northern Flicker, and other woodpeckers.

To make your own suet, cook fat trimmings over low heat until the fat is rendered to liquid. Pour off the liquid into a container (a 16-ounce can is perfect) and put into the refrigerator to set. Discard the solids. Before the suet solidifies, you can mix in seed, nuts, baked beans, stale bread, or small chunks of cheese. Bacon grease also makes good suet.

Homemade suet should be put out only in the winter or when the weather is cool enough to keep it from getting runny or going rancid. Some commercially prepared suet cakes can be put out any time of year.

Another mixture birds like can be made by combining equal parts fat and peanut butter and then stirring in cornmeal until you have a thick paste. You can mix in some of the tidbits mentioned above as well. Spoon the mixture into a suet can or put it into a string bag and hang it from a branch. Another good way to put out this food is in a food log. Use a log 2 or 3 inches in diameter and 12 to 16 inches long. Bore several 1-inch-diameter holes in the log to hold the suet or peanut-butter paste. Drive a heavy screw eye into one end of the log and hang it from a tree.

Stale bread, pastries, skins of baked potatoes, dried cooked spaghetti, cheese, and *cooked* rice (not raw) are among the many kitchen scraps that will attract birds. Put these foods on a platform feeder or in a scrap basket. Soak bread before putting it out. Remove leftover scraps if they begin to spoil.

OPEN PLATFORM: TWO VARIATIONS

A simple platform is among the easiest feeders to make. Here are two variations, one for mounting on a 2 × 2 post or 1-inch pipe and one with short legs for ground-feeding birds.

Make the frames out of 1 × 2s with a half lap cut on each end. Use small nails or $^3/_4$-inch screws to hold the frames together at the corners. The screened floor is sandwiched between two frames with $1^1/_2$-inch screws. A sturdy floor can be made by placing a piece of fine screen over a piece of $^1/_2$- or 1-inch hardware cloth.

The post-version has a 1 × 4 screwed to the bottom of the frame. This is used for attaching a 3- to 5-foot-long 2 × 2 post, which is secured to the frame with four angle brackets. Make a base for the post using 1 × 4s, as shown in the exploded drawing. Alternatively, you can set the post (or threaded pipe mounted to the frame with a floor flange) into a paint can or similar container and fill it with concrete.

The ground version has the same frame mounted on 1 × 2s, with an optional perch.

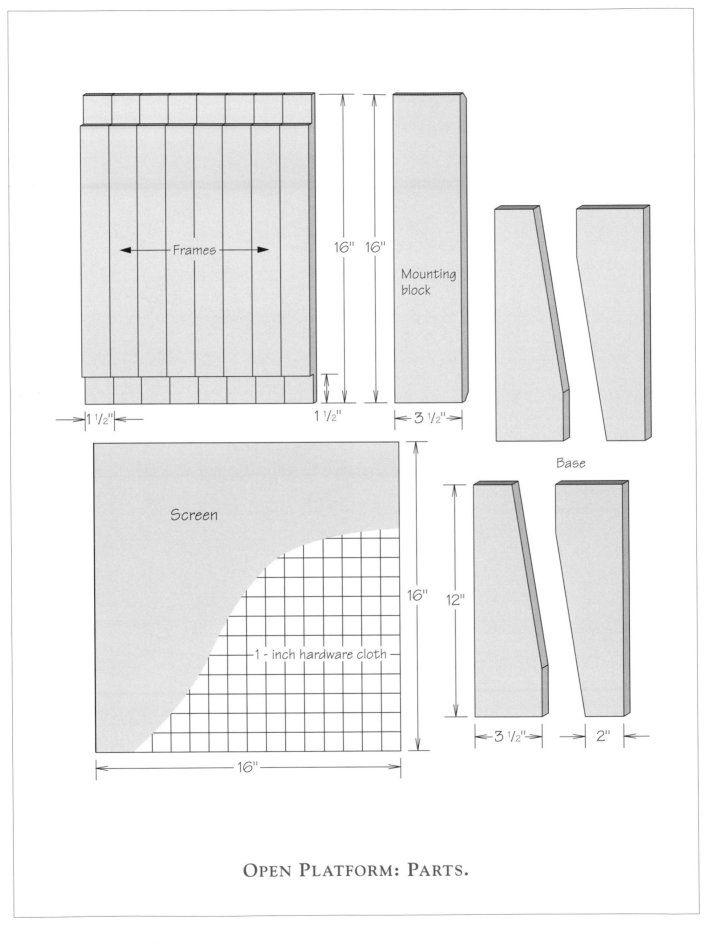

Frames

16" 16"

Mounting
block

1 ½"

1 ½"

3 ½"

Base

Screen

16"

12"

1 - inch hardware cloth

16"

3 ½"

2"

OPEN PLATFORM: PARTS.

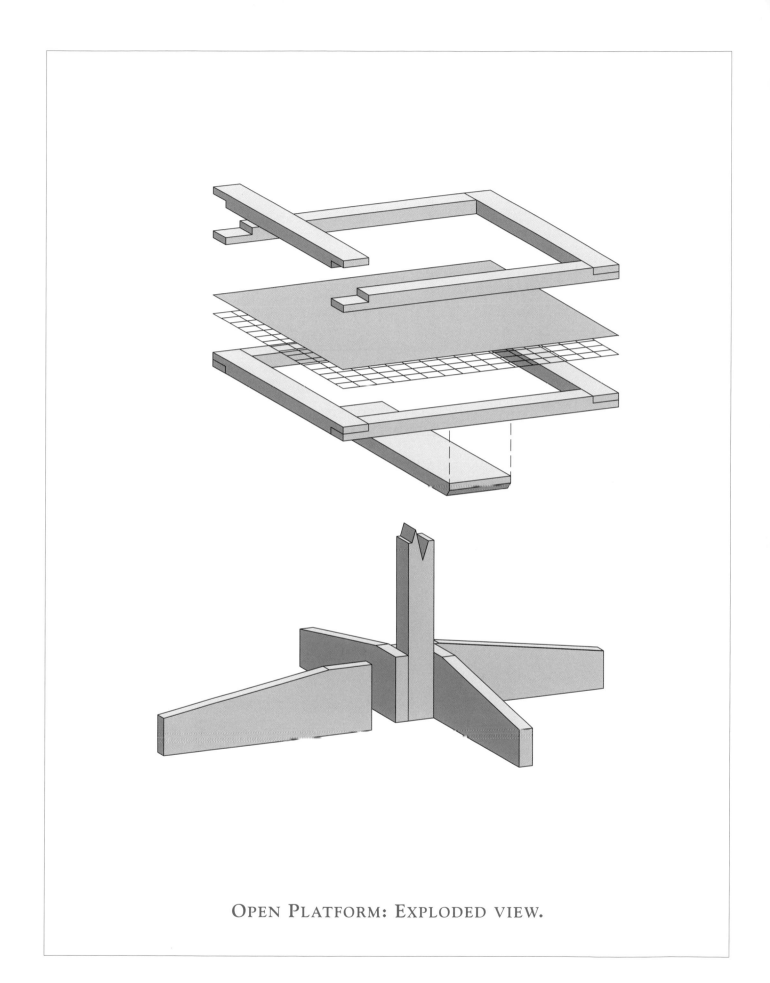

OPEN PLATFORM: EXPLODED VIEW.

OPEN PLATFORM: GROUND VERSION.

COVERED PLATFORM

You can use plywood or solid wood to make the roof of this covered platform feeder. An easy method is to use two pieces of cedar hip and ridge, a roofing material made of two pieces of shingle or shake stapled together at an angle. Look for it at lumberyards or home-improvement centers. It's used to cover ridges and hips on cedar roofs, and you might be able to find discarded pieces at a construction site. You can also use a piece of sheet metal. If cedar roofs are popular in your area, you might be able to find discarded pieces at a construction site.

To build the covered platform, first lay out the sides according to the dimensions shown in the illustration. These dimensions are easily variable, depending on the material you use for the roof. Use a jig saw to cut the pieces. Cut the ridge, rails, and bottom.

Attach the rails to the bottom with 1¹/₄-inch screws or 3d galvanized box nails. Drill pilot holes to prevent the wood from splitting. Attach each side to the bottom with two 1¹/₂-inch screws. Center the ridge between the sides and secure it with a pair of screws or nails at each end. Don't forget the pilot holes. Bore four ¹/₄-inch diameter holes near each corner of the floor for drainage.

Using the roofing material of your choice, cover the platform. Fasten the roof with small galvanized nails. Drive a screw eye through the top and into each side for hanging the feeder from a cord.

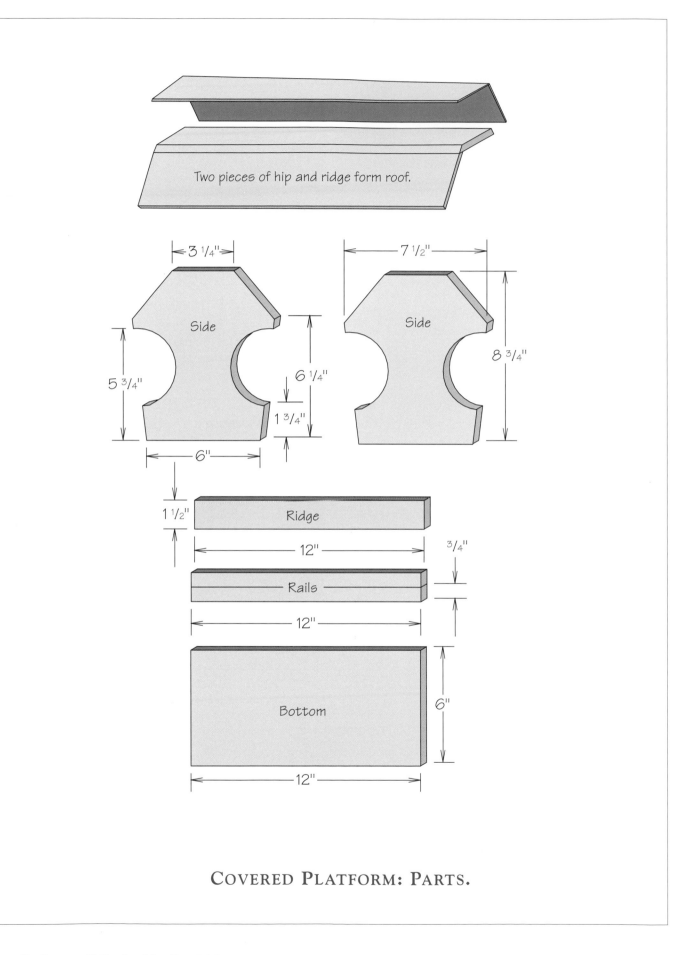

Two pieces of hip and ridge form roof.

3 1/4"

Side

5 3/4"

6 1/4"

1 3/4"

6"

7 1/2"

Side

8 3/4"

1 1/2"

Ridge

12"

3/4"

Rails

12"

Bottom

6"

12"

COVERED PLATFORM: PARTS.

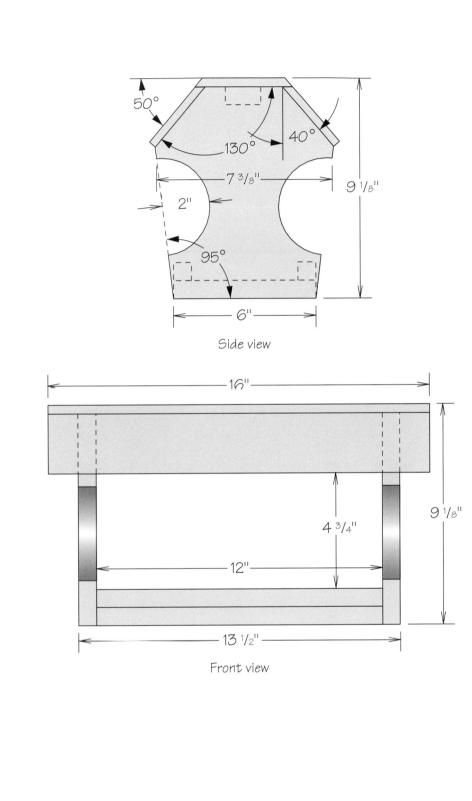

50°

40°

130°

7 ³/₈"

2"

9 ¹/₈"

95°

6"

Side view

16"

9 ¹/₈"

4 ³/₄"

12"

13 ¹/₂"

Front view

COVERED PLATFORM: VIEWS.

COVERED PLATFORM: EXPLODED VIEW.

CHALET SEED FEEDER

The drawback of platform feeders is that they must be replenished often, perhaps even every day. Hopper-style feeders can be loaded up with seed to maintain a constant supply of food for up to several days. The chalet model shown here is a popular one. It features two acrylic panels to contain and dispense the seed and an acrylic floor.

To build the feeder, cut all the parts to the dimensions shown in the illustration. Before cutting the tray frame pieces to length, make a $1/4$-inch-deep saw kerf down the center of the three main pieces. Assemble these pieces with two small screws or nails in each corner. Always drill pilot holes first. Fasten the two thinner pieces to the front of the tray frame with one screw or nail in each end. Cut a piece of acrylic to fit into the channels in the tray sides. You can make a little turnbutton to hold the floor in place.

Make a $1/4$-inch-deep saw kerf about $1/4$ inch in from the edges of each side. Also bore a $1/4$-inch-diameter hole about 1 inch down from the apex of each side. Use two $1^{3}/8$-inch screws to attach each side to the tray. Drive the screws above the tray's centerline so that they don't interfere with the tray floor.

Fasten the top rails with two screws driven through the rail and into the sides. Cut the acrylic panels to fit and slip them into place.

Fasten the roof sections together with three screws or nails. Center the roof assembly on the feeder and transfer the location of each side to the ridge. Bore two $1/4$-inch-diameter holes through the roof. String a length of heavy cord through the roof and each side, knotting each end on the inside of the feeder. The cord will hold the roof in place while the feeder is hanging, but will allow it to move out of the way to fill the hopper.

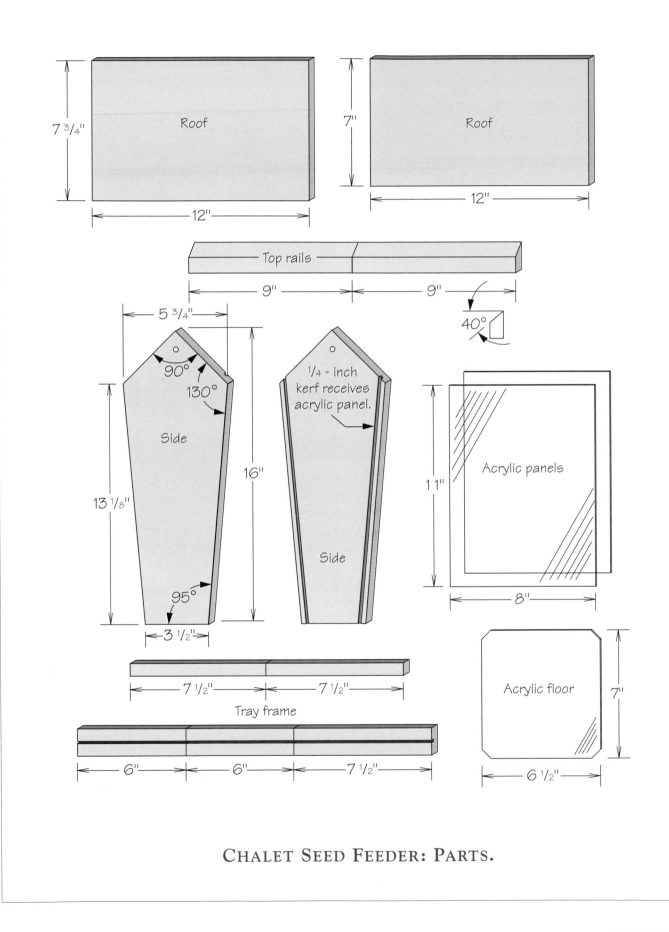

CHALET SEED FEEDER: PARTS.

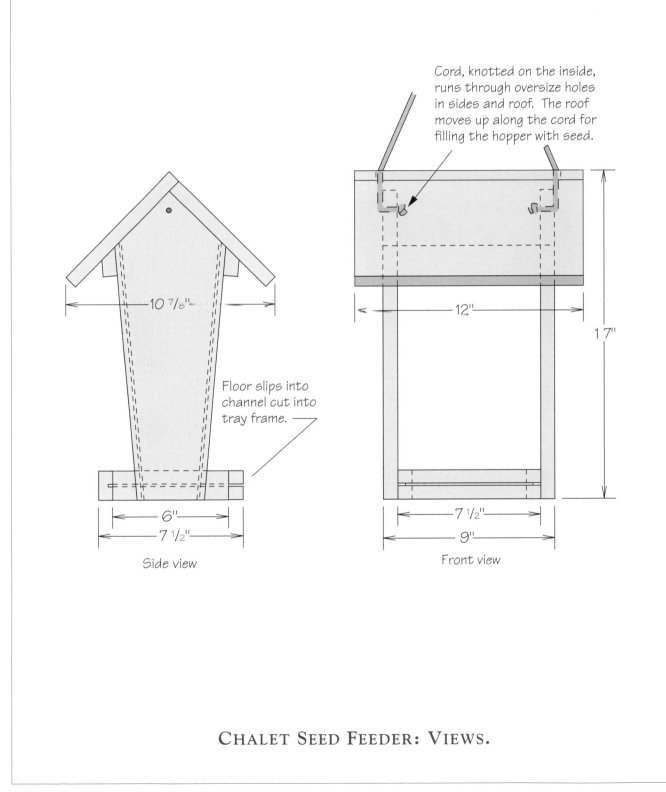

Cord, knotted on the inside, runs through oversize holes in sides and roof. The roof moves up along the cord for filling the hopper with seed.

10 ⅞"

Floor slips into channel cut into tray frame.

6"

7 ½"

Side view

12"

17"

7 ½"

9"

Front view

CHALET SEED FEEDER: VIEWS.

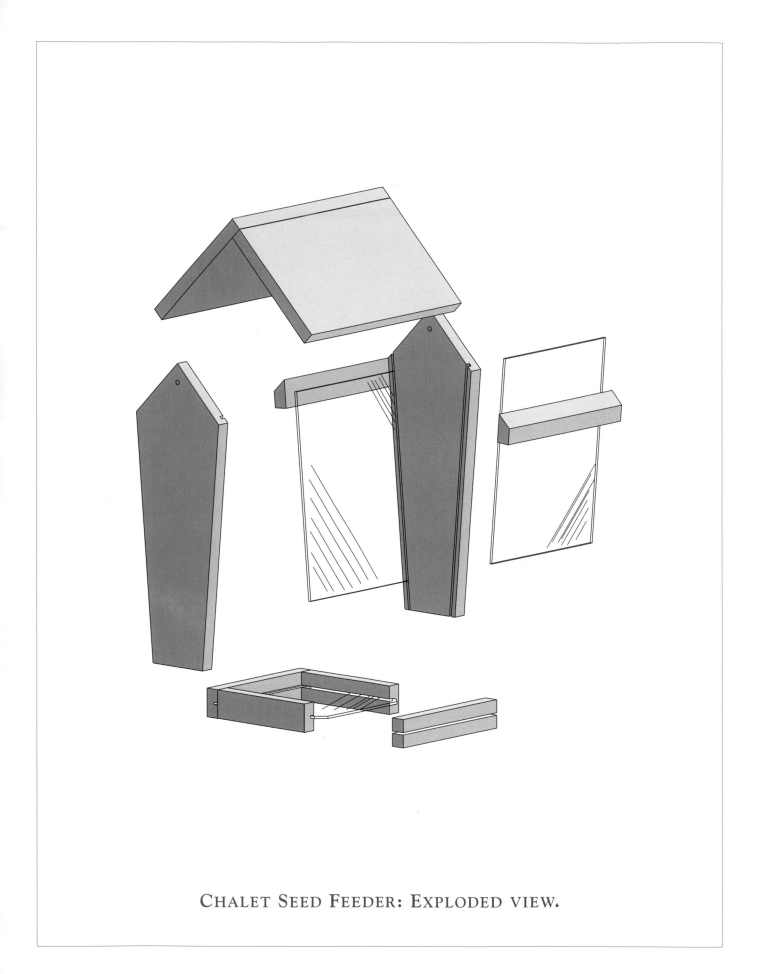

CHALET SEED FEEDER: EXPLODED VIEW.

THISTLE SEED FEEDER

The thistle feeder is designed for the tiny thistle, or niger seed, a favorite of goldfinches. It features six feeding ports. Like the chalet feeder, this one has acrylic panels for viewing the amount of seed available, but it is not self-dispensing. The feeding ports are covered on the inside with $1/8$-inch hardware cloth or other mesh of a size that will contain the seed yet still allow the birds to get at it. Caution: Never use a mesh that can entangle the bird.

Cut out all the parts for the thistle feeder according to the dimensions shown in the illustration. You can use a solid wood or plywood for the top, bottom, bottom retainer, and sides, but it's best to use a $3/4$- or $1/2$-inch piece of plywood for the top retainer. Cutting such a relatively large hole in a piece of solid wood will decrease its strength significantly.

Make a $1/4$-inch-deep saw kerf about $1/4$ inch in from the edges of each side and bore the 2-inch-diameter holes. Also bore the $1/4$-inch diameter holes for the perches. Staple the $1/8$-inch hardware cloth or screen to the inside of each side so that they cover the feeding ports. Push $2 3/4$-inch lengths of $1/4$-inch-diameter dowel into position under the two upper ports. If they don't fit snugly, use a little glue to hold them in place.

Use $1 1/4$-inch screws or 3d galvanized box nails to attach the sides to the bottom and top retainers—two in the top and two in the bottom. It's important to use pilot holes in both sides and retainers, which are susceptible to splitting. Use four screws to attach the bottom, driving them up through the bottom and into the sides, being careful to avoid the screws that hold the retainer.

Next, locate and install the two screw eyes at the top of the feeder. Put the top in place and mark it with the relative positions of the screw eyes. Bore two $1/4$-inch-diameter holes through the top. Run a length of heavy cord through the holes and screw eyes and secure each end with a knot. The top will stay in place while the feeder is hanging, but you can move it out of the way to fill the feeder with thistle seed.

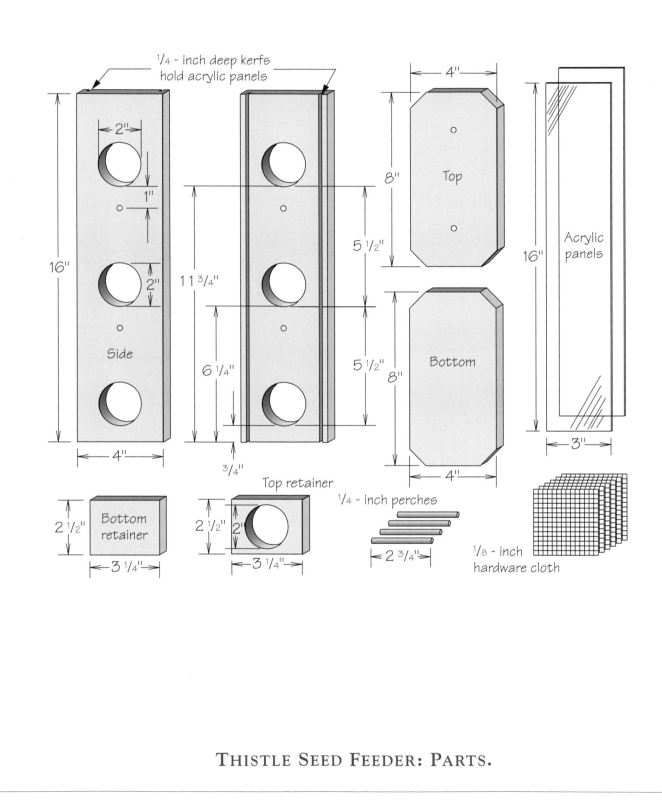

¼ - inch deep kerfs
hold acrylic panels

2"

1"

2"

16"

11 ¾"

6 ¼"

Side

4"

¾"

5 ½"

5 ½"

4"

8"

Top

Bottom

8"

4"

16"

Acrylic
panels

3"

Top retainer

2 ½"

Bottom
retainer

3 ¼"

2 ½"

2"

3 ¼"

¼ - inch perches

2 ¾"

⅛ - inch
hardware cloth

THISTLE SEED FEEDER: PARTS.

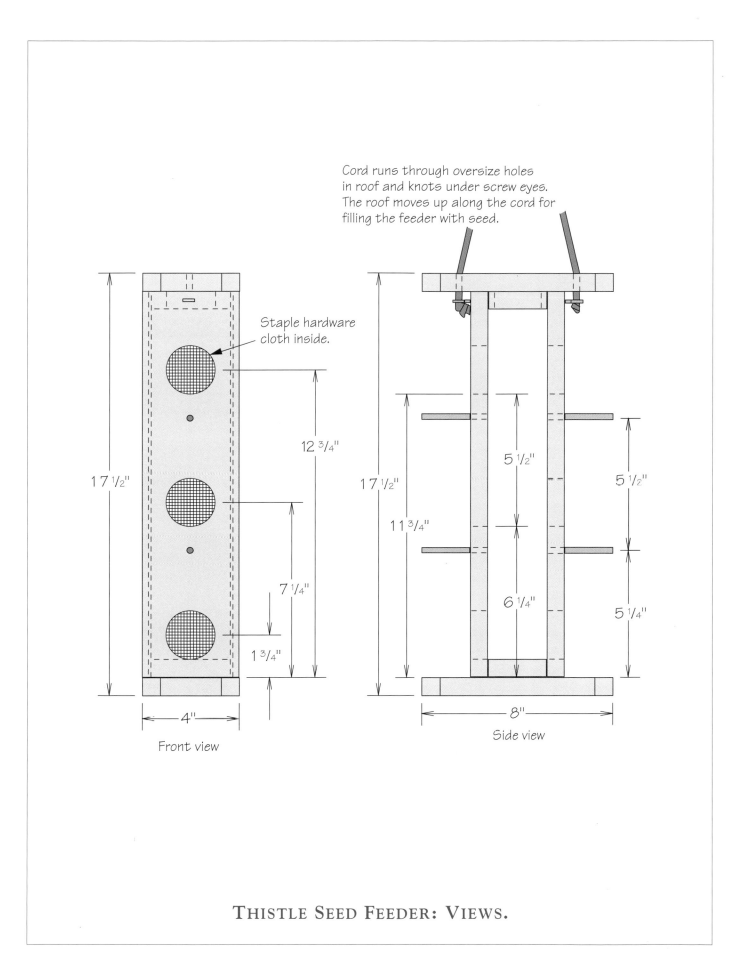

Cord runs through oversize holes
in roof and knots under screw eyes.
The roof moves up along the cord for
filling the feeder with seed.

Staple hardware
cloth inside.

17 1/2"

12 3/4"

7 1/4"

1 3/4"

4"

Front view

17 1/2"

11 3/4"

5 1/2"

6 1/4"

5 1/2"

5 1/4"

8"

Side view

THISTLE SEED FEEDER: VIEWS.

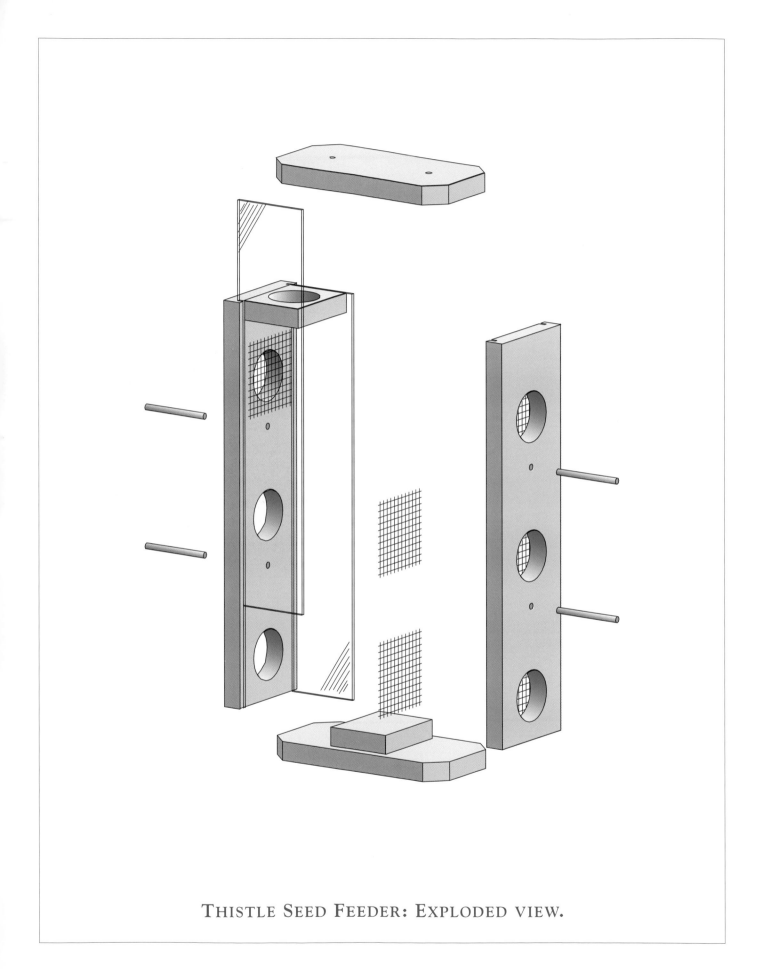

THISTLE SEED FEEDER: EXPLODED VIEW.

SUET CAN HOLDER

Here's a perfect holder for your homemade suet. The can into which you pour the renderings fits into the holder. The illustration shows a 16-ounce can, but any small or medium-size can will do. Check the rim of the can carefully for any sharp edges and file them down. On a backing board of suitable size, trace around the can end. Place one 5-inch and two 7-inch dowels equidistant around the perimeter of the circle. The two lower pegs are extra long to serve as perches. The holder can be mounted or hung just about anywhere. You can make the dowels twice as long and mount a can on the back side too. Suspend this double holder from a branch.

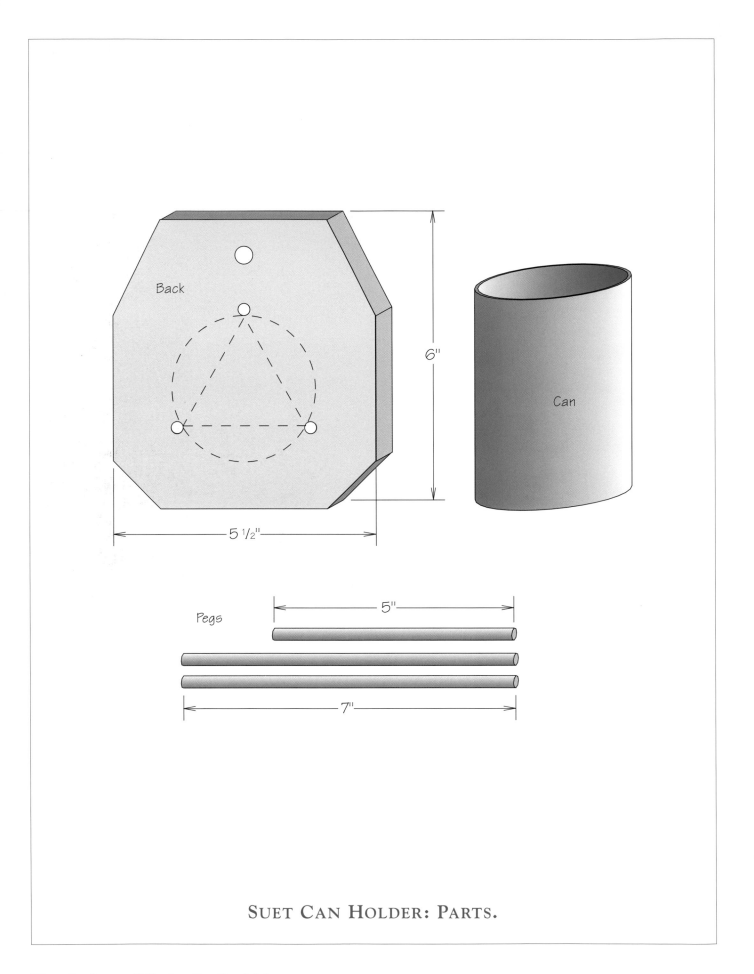

Back

6"

5 ½"

Can

Pegs

5"

7"

SUET CAN HOLDER: PARTS.

SCRAP AND SUET BASKET

You can toss your kitchen scraps out into the yard, but placing them in a basket is a little more elegant. Use 1-inch hardware cloth, chicken wire, or other heavy mesh for the basket. Round off the corners of the side pieces with a belt sander to make it easier to bend the hardware cloth around them. Fasten the mesh to the wooden frame with small galvanized fencing staples.

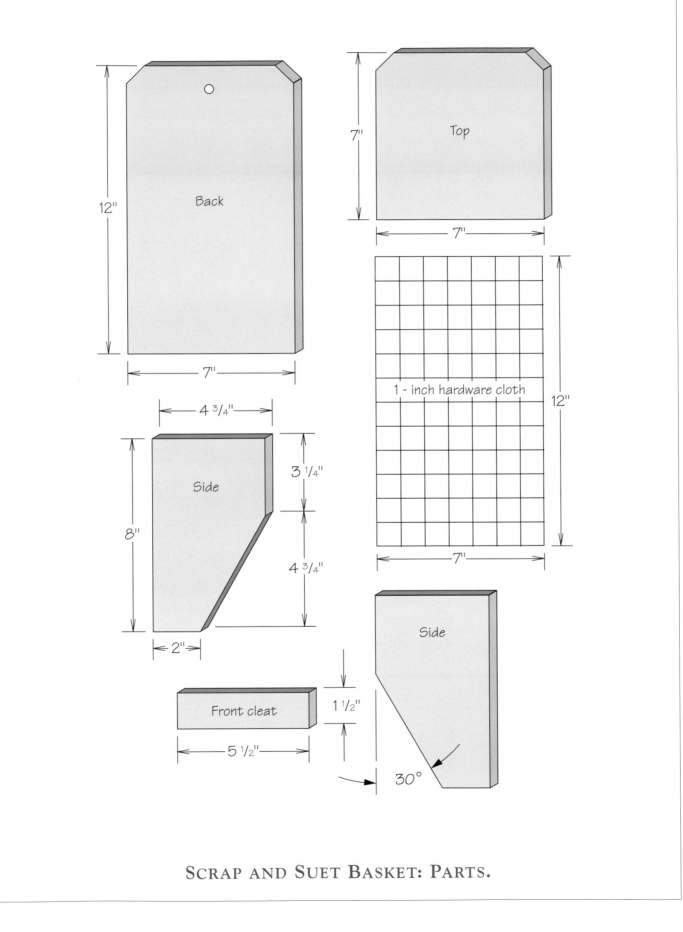

12"

Back

7"

7"

Top

7"

4 3/4"

Side

3 1/4"

8"

4 3/4"

2"

1 - inch hardware cloth

12"

7"

Side

Front cleat

1 1/2"

5 1/2"

30°

SCRAP AND SUET BASKET: PARTS.

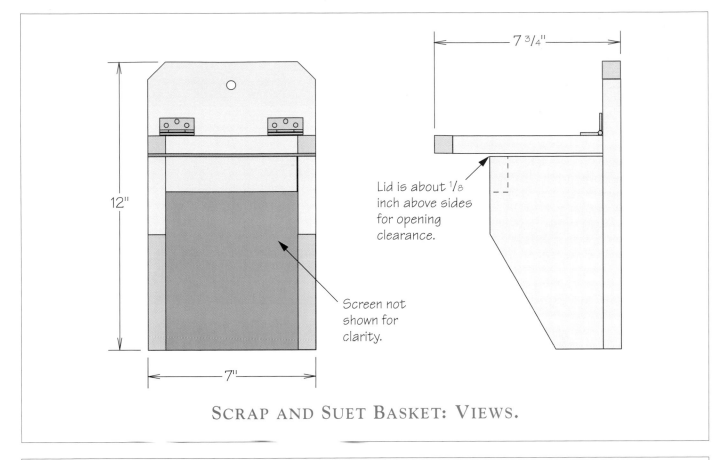

12"

7 3/4"

Lid is about 1/8 inch above sides for opening clearance.

Screen not shown for clarity.

7"

SCRAP AND SUET BASKET: VIEWS.

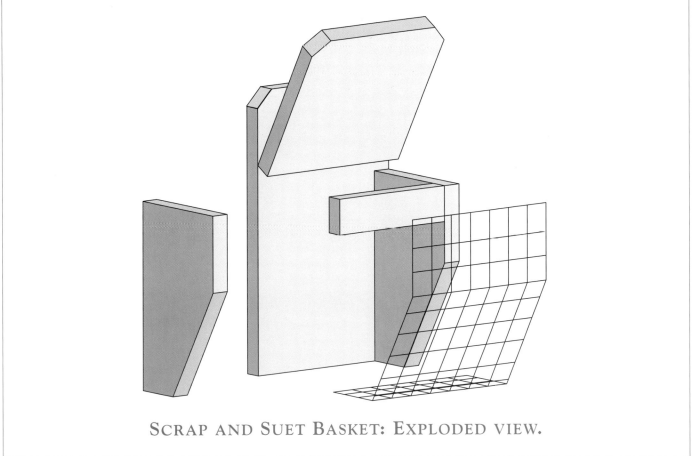

SCRAP AND SUET BASKET: EXPLODED VIEW.

BIBLIOGRAPHY

Burton, Robert. *Concise Birdfeeder Handbook: A Guide to Attracting and Observing Birds*. New York: DK Publications, 1992.

Campbell, Scott D. *The Complete Book of Birdhouse Construction for Woodworkers*. New York: Dover Publications, 1984.

————. *Easy-to-Make Bird Feeders for Woodworkers*. New York: Dover Publications, 1989.

Gardner, John F. *Backyard Birdfeeding*. Mechanicsburg, PA: Stackpole Books, 1996.

Self, Charles R. *Making Birdhouses and Feeders*. New York: Sterling Publishing Co., 1985.

Shalaway, Scott. *A Guide to Bird Homes*. Marietta, Ohio: Bird Watcher's Digest Press, 1995.

Stokes, Donald, and Lillian Stokes. *Complete Birdhouse Book*. Boston: Little Brown, 1990.

METRIC CONVERSIONS

INCHES TO MILLIMETERS

IN.	MM	IN.	MM
1	25.4	51	1295.4
2	50.8	52	1320.8
3	76.2	53	1346.2
4	101.6	54	1371.6
5	127.0	55	1397.0
6	152.4	56	1422.4
7	177.8	57	1447.8
8	203.2	58	1473.2
9	228.6	59	1498.6
10	254.0	60	1524.0
11	279.4	61	1549.4
12	304.8	62	1574.8
13	330.2	63	1600.2
14	355.6	64	1625.6
15	381.0	65	1651.0
16	406.4	66	1676.4
17	431.8	67	1701.8
18	457.2	68	1727.2
19	482.6	69	1752.6
20	508.0	70	1778.0
21	533.4	71	1803.4
22	558.8	72	1828.8
23	584.2	73	1854.2
24	609.6	74	1879.6
25	635.0	75	1905.0
26	660.4	76	1930.4
27	685.8	77	1955.8
28	711.2	78	1981.2
29	736.6	79	2006.6
30	762.0	80	2032.0
31	787.4	81	2057.4
32	812.8	82	2082.8
33	838.2	83	2108.2
34	863.6	84	2133.6
35	889.0	85	2159.0
36	914.4	86	2184.4
37	939.8	87	2209.8
38	965.2	88	2235.2
39	990.6	89	2260.6
40	1016.0	90	2286.0
41	1041.4	91	2311.4
42	1066.8	92	2336.8
43	1092.2	93	2362.2
44	1117.6	94	2387.6
45	1143.0	95	2413.0
46	1168.4	96	2438.4
47	1193.8	97	2463.8
48	1219.2	98	2489.2
49	1244.6	99	2514.6
50	1270.0	100	2540.0

The above table is exact on the basis: 1 in. = 25.4 mm

U.S. TO METRIC

1 inch	=	2.540 centimeters
1 foot	=	.305 meter
1 yard	=	.914 meter
1 mile	=	1.609 kilometers

METRIC TO U.S.

1 millimeter	=	.039 inch
1 centimeter	=	.394 inch
1 meter	=	3.281 feet or 1.094 yards
1 kilometer	=	.621 mile

INCH-METRIC EQUIVALENTS

Fraction	Decimal Equivalent Customary (IN.)	Metric (MM)	Fraction	Decimal Equivalent Customary (IN.)	Metric (MM)
$1/64$	.015	0.3969	$33/64$	.515	13.0969
$1/32$	.031	0.7938	$17/32$	.531	13.4938
$3/64$	.046	1.1906	$35/64$	.546	13.8906
$1/16$	.062	1.5875	$9/16$	.562	14.2875
$5/64$	.078	1.9844	$37/64$	.578	14.6844
$3/32$	.093	2.3813	$19/32$	.593	15.0813
$7/64$	.109	2.7781	$39/64$	.609	15.4781
$1/8$	.125	3.1750	$5/8$	.625	15.8750
$9/64$	.140	3.5719	$41/64$	.640	16.2719
$5/32$	.156	3.9688	$21/32$	.656	16.6688
$11/64$	.171	4.3656	$43/64$	.671	17.0656
$3/16$	.187	4.7625	$11/16$	.687	17.4625
$13/64$	.203	5.1594	$45/64$	.703	17.8594
$7/32$	.218	5.5563	$23/32$	.718	18.2563
$15/64$	.234	5.9531	$47/64$	.734	18.6531
$1/4$	.250	6.3500	$3/4$	.750	19.0500
$17/64$	.265	6.7469	$49/64$	.765	19.4469
$9/32$	.281	7.1438	$25/32$	.781	19.8438
$19/64$	.296	7.5406	$51/64$	.796	20.2406
$5/16$	.312	7.9375	$13/16$	.812	20.6375
$21/64$	.328	8.3384	$53/64$	.828	21.0344
$11/32$	.343	8.7313	$27/32$	.843	21.4313
$23/64$	.359	9.1281	$55/64$	.859	21.8281
$3/8$	.375	9.5250	$7/8$	.875	22.2250
$25/64$	.390	9.9219	$57/64$	.890	22.6219
$13/32$	.406	10.3188	$29/32$	.906	23.0188
$27/64$	.421	10.7156	$59/64$	.921	23.4156
$7/16$	.437	11.1125	$15/16$	.937	23.8125
$29/64$	.453	11.5094	$61/64$	.953	24.2094
$15/32$	.468	11.9063	$31/32$	.968	24.6063
$31/64$	.484	12.3031	$63/64$	.984	25.0031
$1/2$	.500	12.7000	1	1.000	25.4000

INDEX

Page numbers in italics indicate tables and illustrations